# Silver Linings

## Finding my way through life's storms

By

Phoebe Walker

Phoebe Walker

# Advanced thoughts about
# Silver Linings, Finding my way through life's storms.

"In Silver Linings: Finding my way through Life's Storms, Phoebe Walker courageously shares her life's journey with others. It is sensitive and insightful, and serves as a beacon of hope for others who have their own crosses to bear".

> — Scott Sullivan, MD, FACS,
> Center for Restorative Breast Surgery,
> New Orleans, LA.

"I don't usually read books from this genus. I typically read books on science fiction, history, and war. However, I was pleasantly surprised how this book kept my interest at all times. Phoebe is an excellent writer and funny too. Once I started reading, I could not put the book down. She managed to find a way to take the most horrific life situations and through faith, managed to pull herself out while somehow experiencing humor. I purchased this book after my cancer returned and found me on hospice care. Phoebe's deep faith and optimism were strengths that have had a priceless impact on my final days."

> — George Wayne Ricks, CPA
> Titusville, FL.

"Silver Linings: Finding my way through life's storms, is a deeply moving work about one woman's journey through an abusive childhood, a happy marriage, and a terrifying health crisis. Gretchen writes with honesty and an open heart, sharing her deepest thoughts, darkest moments, scariest fears, and most intimate details candidly and honestly. Hers is a story that is riveting, honest, and inspiring. I gasped many times at the dark episodes in her life and cheered for the victories they produced. I guarantee that readers will be inspired by her story — I know I have been."

— Cynthia Furlong Reynolds
Author/Editor/Speaker

"Gretchen Walker was a CU biology graduate who has had more than her share of medical struggles. When she was here, she completed one of the best independent studies I have ever mentored. Her work resulted in awards and publications in spite of her health obstacles. I applaud this "Little engine that could." After reading her book you too will see that she's a gentle spirit with a dragon heart!!! She is a prime example of no limitations."

— Dr. Gordon Weddle, PhD.
Biology professor
Campbellsville University, KY

"Phoebe's story is an inspiration for us all. I have personally witnessed some of her struggles since we met approximately twelve years ago. Her strength, talent, compassion for others, hard work and faith are assets we all should strive for in our own lives."

— David G. Daly, D.C.,

Daly Chiropractic and Wellness Center,

Titusville, FL.

Phoebe Walker

# Silver Linings

## Finding my way through life's storms

## Phoebe Walker

### A true survivor's story!

Phoebe Walker

ISBN - 10: 0-692-95373-6

ISBN – 13: 978-0-692-95373-0

Cover design by: Phoebe Walker
Edited by: Cynthia Furlong Reynolds

Credits:
Maya Angelou Quote used with permission by Caged Bird Legacy, LLC.
Quote from First Aid Kits' song "My Silver Lining," is used with permission by Coda Agency.

# Acknowledgements

In loving memory of my little angel,

Zoey. You were my best silver lining imaginable. In the darkest days,

you didn't make life easier, you made it possible!

Thank you sunshine.

May 29, 2004 – February 15, 2017

This was my Zoey sitting, next to me sharing the seatbelt, August
2016. That was her favorite place to ride.

# Contents

This photo was taken in March 2013, by my
friend Wanda, as one of my graduation picture
for graduate school.

Phoebe Walker

# Prologue

My first book, *The Silver Lining Encounters with Angels,* was not an easy book for me to write because I discussed some deeply personal details from my life. Many of them my birth family did not learn about until after the book was released. What greatly influenced my decision to write that book was my belief that all of us have at least one chapter in our book of life that we would rather not read aloud. In my case, I have more chapters than I can count. By allowing myself to become fully exposed, I attained a level of personal healing while aiming to help others find their own hope, inspriation, joy, and sense of direction. That goal made sharing my story fully worth my absolute exposure.

Over the past two years I've received overwhelming response from readers. They shared endless appreciation for my decision to share my story, explaining that it helped them in their lives in significant ways. The one major and constant concern I heard was the Christian-based language and focus in my first book. I took that concern to heart and decided that in order to reach more people, I needed to rework my book.

God clearly remains my source of strength. However, as you read this book, I want *you* to be able to identify *your* peronal source of hope, inspiration, strength, and faith, whatever it may be. So here's the fully revised book with updated information, since new developments have taken place since the first edition.

In this book, I share how I identified silver linings and used them as lifesavers to pull me out of my life storms. At the root of every success was perseverance. When I learned to dance through life's storms, I enabled myself to embrace freedom from the oppressing elements of each trial, one at a time. My hope is that no matter how dark your trials get, you too will be able to look up and find your own silver linings.

In the difficulties of life, I have found that sometimes we need to give ourselves permission to wallow in the trials for a night (or a couple of days), but then we need to get up, brush off our rear ends, and set new goals—and then work towards those goals. But let's face it: most of us can't get from our rear ends to a standing position in a single move. Likewise, it often takes many steps to successfully transform trials into into triumphs. This book clearly relays a pattern from my own life: I wallow, silver linings are revealed, and through them I become motivated to move forward. I encourage you to not lose your momentum. If that happens, it's time to assess what went wrong and try again.

Throughout this book you will see me make reference to medical procedures and diseases. I am not an expert in either of these areas. What I have written here is solely based on my personal experiences. Please do not take my references as expert advice.

Lastly, when reading about silver linings, keep in mind what I have learned: silver linings will probably be different for each situation. Most of all, realize that it takes a hardship or trial to recognize our need for a silver lining—and to recognize that they exist in our everyday lives, too.

I bid you well on your search for your own silver linings. May my examples prepare you to better identify them in your time of need.

Aloha and Namaste!

Phoebe

# My Silver Lining

*"Having no idea who or what or where I am.*

*Something good comes with the bad.*

*A song's never just sad.*

*There's hope, there's a silver lining.*

*Show me my silver lining...*

*... Show me my silver lining, I try to keep on keeping on."*

Song and lyrics by First Aid Kit

Then, as you keep on keeping on,

*"Do the best you can until you know better.*

*Then when you know better, do better.*

- Maya Angelou

# Chapter 1
# In the Beginning, Finding me

"Gretchen, do you know Christ?" My best friend, Cristi asked, sitting on her bed in the semi-darkness of a sleepover after my sophomore year in high school. The question sparked a personal reflection. I'd weathered sixteen years of hardships on my own—my mother's constant verbal and physical abuse, promiscuity, bullies in elementary school—could I use an ally like God to walk with me through the next sixteen years? My answer? Most definitely *yes*.

Early in June 1989, Cristi guided me through my first spiritual life change. It was a decision that I believe held deep eternal reward and changed the course of my life forever. First, let me rewind to tell a little about how I reached that moment.

My earliest memories date back to when I was my daddy's three-year-old little princess. I am amazed to look back now and think of how much my three-year-old mind could already comprehend the lack of love from one parent—namely, my mother. I believe that realization not only created a deep confusion that lasted throughout my young life, it also caused a peculiarity in my persona. The only person who seemed to stabilize me was my dad. I can say with all certainty that he was my first silver lining.

My daddy called me his "little pinky" because I was tiny and wanted everything to be pink, even, at times, my food. My dad had a short, stocky body shape, but I looked up to him as if he had the strong, noble stature suited for a king. He did not have great physical strength, but he certainly had a strong and tenacious voice. However, when he handled me in my younger years, he did so with a nurturing, gentle, and loving touch. I believe those traits were necessary for him to protect his little princess. Me.

My dad was the pastor of an older Presbyterian church that was located directly across the street from our house. I thought that old church looked just like a gigantic castle, which made it easy for me to fantasize about my childhood. I made my daddy the ruler over the castle and the kingdom that surrounded it. Of course, in my little mind, the entire kingdom only stretched to the block that surrounded the church and the block that surrounded our house.

My grandma on my dad's side knew I was the child who needed a bit more attention. While I did not intentionally seek it, my subconscious must have made it evident to her, because every time I saw her, she intentionally made private time for the two of us. This occurred about once a year and sometimes twice, until she passed away. I imagine her understanding and caring contributed to my above-average excitement about visiting with her.

Our alone time generally started with me sitting in her lap, the two of us in her rocking chair—yes, even after I became an adult. She proceeded to rock with me while gently patting my bum. As we rocked, she told me a story, always the same one. The story of my parents' lives went something like this:

*Years ago, a handsome young man found his beautiful maiden. They fell in love and married. Several years later, the fair maiden gave birth to a beautiful baby girl, whom they cherished together.* [She was my older sister.]

*Three years later, that same maiden went to the hospital to give birth to their second child. She delivered a bouncing baby boy. What joy! She had the perfect family, with one boy and one girl. A few minutes later, to the couple's surprise and shock, the maiden went into labor again and delivered another child. A beautiful baby girl. The maiden did not know she had been pregnant with twins until that moment.*

*You would have thought the young mother would be overjoyed with another baby, but that little girl did not get the same reception as her twin brother. In fact, the mother focused most of her attention on the older sister and the twin brother. I know you must be feeling badly for that sweet little bundle of joy, but you should not, for she had a daddy who went to her side whenever he felt she needed him. That man loved all three of his children very dearly, but he also knew the last of his children was delicate and needed him in a different way than her siblings did. For this reason, he spent a little extra time with this one...*

After my grandmother finished the story, she would give me a big squeeze, kiss me on the head, and say, "This is the story of your family. *You* are the youngest baby girl." Of course, she adapted the story many years later, after my two half-brothers came along, when I officially became the middle child.

My grandmother was very open about telling me that I was born to be a special gift for my dad. She reminded me of this fact until she died, the year I turned thirty. In fact, she was not the only one who alluded to that story over the years. Family members on both sides told me that they remember my dad taking care of me the majority of the time when I was an infant and toddler.

When I think back to my early memories, when my daddy figured as the king of my life, my mother was always the bad person. In fact, many times I looked at her as the wicked stepmother or witch who only wished to do me harm. While I desperately wanted a "mommy", I was afraid of my own mother and almost daily went to Dad to tell on her, describing how she was so mean to me. I used to dream that somehow she would go away and a nice sweet mommy would replace her, so you can imagine what went through my head when my parents announced they were getting divorced four years later, the summer I turned seven.

I blamed myself for wishing they would split up. I felt I was responsible for breaking up the family. I wondered how anyone could love me after I caused so much brokenness. Fortunately, I could talk to my paternal grandmother. She was like my fairy godmother and always knew the right things to say to make me feel better. Grandma was my second silver lining.

After I heard about the divorce, I called Grandma to talk about it. She said, "Listen to what I am about to tell you, and never forget.

This situation is *not* your fault. You are more special than you can ever know." She went on to remind me that my mother was so focused on my brother and sister that my dad had become my primary care giver, at least every time Grandma saw us. He had enough love for me to cover both parents, she assured me. "You were made for him," she said.

That rationale made sense to me. I remembered strangers commenting that I must not have had any legs of my own because my daddy was always carrying me. Then, when I finally let him put me down, I clung to his legs so I could hide behind them, if necessary.

After my parents divorced in 1980, my brother, sister, and I moved into a two-story apartment in Indianapolis with our mom. Have you ever been in a situation so dreadful that you wanted to hold your breath until you got through it? Well, that was how I felt for the next five years spent in that apartment. Both my brother and sister had friends and spent as much time away from home as they could. I spent the majority of time at the apartment because I had no friends nearby.

After the divorce, my mother became a very angry person, and she vented her anger by yelling all the time and by physical brutality. My sister was the oldest child, so our mother leveraged many of her responsibilities onto my sister, including dinner preparations and care for my brother and me.

Any time something went wrong with my sister's handling of those added responsibilities, our mother went after her. She used my sister's long hair as a tool to smash her against the wall. Once pinned in a corner, my sister would brace herself, using her arms to protect her body and shield her head while our mother proceeded to punch and kick her. Whenever I saw or heard this happening, I ran to the dark corner in my room and sobbed. It was a constant reminder of how little control we three children had in our lives. There was no escape from our personal hell.

The pretty hedges around the back porch had a sinister meaning for my brother and me. My mother was always finding a reason to order us to cut our own switches from those plants, so she or her boyfriend could whip us with them.

One day my brother and I became so upset about the whippings that we dug up every one of those plants—at least a dozen of them. We not only dug them up, but we ripped all the branches off the main sections, then carried them out the gate and down about 200 feet to the end of the six-foot fence behind our apartment. We stacked the branches behind that fence in a wooded area. When our mother returned home, she became hysterical, crying and screaming. "Those were my favorite plants! They were beautiful and so expensive," she bellowed. They obviously meant more to her than her children did, I realized. You would have thought we crushed her world, she was that angry. I thought she would never stop shouting at us that night.

Unfortunately, removing those hedges did not stop the corporal punishment. She continued using her fists, feet, and kitchen utensils when she was upset. I believe this abuse, coupled with the bullying from kids at school, led to my academic struggles. Many years I barely passed into the next grade.

While we lived at this apartment, I had a very close relationship with my twin brother. I hoped it would always stay that way. Unfortunately, it did not. Thankfully, now that we are older, we are in the process of rebuilding our relationship. I was fortunate to have him in my life. He was a major silver lining for me when we were young.

I oftentimes cried as I watched my twin brother wrongly punished for something he hadn't done. The worst incident was when he decided to take the blame for something I did. I cannot remember what it was that made my mother angry this time, but my brother felt he needed to shield me from her anger. Just days before, she had dragged me up the stairs by my ear while screaming, kicking, and hitting me. "She's going to pull my ear off my head before we reach the top step," I thought to myself through a haze of agony. Days later, my brother knew that I was still suffering a great deal of pain, and he interceded, to protect me from another round of punishment. I was grateful that he wanted to do that for me, but I was terrified about what she would do to him.

My bedroom door was situated all the way to the right on the wall. Directly to the left of the door was the closet my sister and I shared. It had three sliding mirrored doors that stretched the remaining length of that wall. When our mother's explosion began, I was sitting on the floor next to the bedroom door, which was slightly ajar. My legs were stretched along the wall, so my feet were in the closet.

When my mom started punishing my brother for something I had done, I watched the abuse through the pinhole opening of the door. I was terrified, absolutely convinced that my mother was going to kill my brother. Thoughts began spinning in my head about how my brother and I could escape the hell in which we were living—or, better yet, how we could just disappear.

My brother was writhing in the fetal position on the floor next to the stairs while our mother kept kicking and punching him. "Why won't she stop? She's killing him!" Those thoughts bombarded my mind. I could not control my tears and sobs. I wanted to run out and start hitting her to make her stop, but I was frozen in fear. Finally, I heard her footsteps clump down the stairs. I snuck down the hallway to my brother's room to see if he was okay. I found him on his bed inspecting his wounds and bruises. I thanked him with tears in my eyes for taking that lashing, and I explained my sorrow and regret for what he had endured on my behalf.

When I returned to my room, I climbed deep into a corner of my closet, where I hid for protection and cried. I spent many hours at least once a week in that space—whenever my mother vented her anger. The closet was dark and quiet and there I could imagine I was under a cloak of invisibility.

Another hiding place was the floor under my bed. One day I was hiding there, trying to think of other places where I could hide. It was too easy for my mother to look under the bed, grab any one of my appendages, and yank me out. She could also grab me by my hair and pull me out of the closet. That day, I looked up at the base of my box spring and noticed a significant gap in between the springs. I tore a large hole in the liner and climbed feet-first in between a row of springs. I made sure to keep my face towards the ground, so I could always see what was coming. While it was an uncomfortably tight fit, it was a good option for short-term hiding. Yes, I really was that small. My unhealthy weight was a result of an inability to hold food down on most days, a result of the constant stress and fear, I suppose.

For me, it was slim pickings to find friendly girls my age in that apartment complex. In fact, when I could not stand being alone, there was only one girl I could talk to, though she really was a last resort. The one girl I considered a good friend lived about three miles down the road, and that was too far for me to walk. I know this because I tried it once on a school snow day and gave up halfway there.

Most of the other kids at school were brutally mean to me. They made fun of me for the clothes my mom made me wear, which greatly resembled something you would see on the television show "Little House on the Prairie". Everything I had was outdated—embarrassingly so. Unusual clothing is a sure-fire way to catch unwanted attention. I was constantly being bullied. Many times I hoped my brother would protect me, and on several occasions he told those bullies, "Don't say that to her! She's my sister. I'm the only one who's allowed to say those things about her."

However, the school bullies persisted, threatening to meet me after school and beat me up. I was by far the smallest in my class in those days, under four feet tall and weighing less than fifty pounds. I didn't know the first thing about fighting, but I knew that a war was waged against me, both at school and at home.

I finally got tired of the bullying and worked up my courage to meet those girls behind my apartment complex. When the tall skinny girl shoved me, I pushed back. Hard enough for her to fall on the ground and lose her glasses. When she got up, she ran home, with her friends following right behind. They didn't bother me again after that. However, my victories were few and far between during those five years, so I cherished whatever small victories I could manage.

My mother hated my father so much that she manufactured games to torment him, using my siblings and me as pawns. For example, one time my stepmother came to pick us up for the weekend. She parked in front of our apartment and honked her horn instead of walking to the door to get us. Knowing my mother's temperament, I would not have chosen to walk up to our door, either.

I remember feeling a huge sense of relief when I heard the horn because I desperately wanted to leave. But my mom physically blocked the door with her body and told us we were not done with our chores. We were not permitted to leave the house until we completed the work to her unreasonable standards. That only made me work faster.

Our stepmom waited over thirty minutes and then drove the half-hour back home to get my father. When he arrived at our apartment, he was livid. We missed the meal that night at Dad's house, thanks to our mother's behavior. We were sent to bed after a dinner of toast, water, and vitamins. I questioned why we even went to his house for visitation. After all, we were only there for two nights and he was sending us to bed unreasonably early for the first night. Where is the visitation in that?

Lying in bed that night, I remember feeling so angry with both of my parents. Why didn't Dad understand that it was Mom's fault, not ours? Why did Mom hate us so much? Why did Dad seem happier with his new family than with us? I didn't understand the dynamics then, but the reality is that this type of event occurred not because of anything my siblings and I had done, but because of the animosity my parents had for each other. We were pawns in the hate game.

I cannot begin to describe how much I hated life between the second and sixth grades. At least once a year, I attempted to move in with my dad, but my mom would never let that happen. Whenever my efforts failed, I tried running away, but I didn't know where to run. More times than I can count, I thought about living in that wooded area behind our apartment complex, but I knew there were devil worshipers who set up shrines out there, and they terrified me as much as my mother did. I finally conceded to bide my time and wait until the day I could move in with my dad.

After living in the apartment complex for five years, my mom married her boyfriend and we all moved to Lebanon, Indiana. That was in 1985, just as I was starting seventh grade. The house we moved into belonged to my mom's new husband. I was relieved to have a new start, with so many other kids who were new to the same school. My brother and I naturally migrated into the new-student group. Unfortunately, my brother and I became so active with friends that we didn't talk the way we used to.

I tried to develop a relationship with my sister, thinking it would be easy because we were older now and still shared a room. I remember watching her and daydreaming about what it would be like to be her. She had a car. She was an honors student at the high school. She worked when she was not participating in school activities. The car and the job gave my sister independence, which I believed made her life better than mine. I hoped that if I followed in her steps, I might be able to escape the hell I was living.

Many years later, as adults, my sister shared with me how difficult her life had been in those days. She described scenarios and details that I had suppressed for years, yet retrieved easily. She explained that being old enough to work put her in a better position to escape our *house of horrors* as soon as possible, and she grasped the opportunity. That explained why I didn't see her often. Today, I'm pleased to say that we actively connect with each other.

Fortunately, it didn't take me long to develop genuine relationships at school with a small group of friends. Kids at Lebanon Middle School were not mean like those in my Indianapolis school. Although the popular kids still treated me as a dork and a nerd, my friends treated me well, so the rude gestures and comments from the popular kids didn't bother me as much. I knew my friends had an abundance of love for me, and that gave me a sense of belonging with them. This group of friends formed my next silver lining. I do not believe I would have had the strength to function in that season of my life if not for them.

What bothered me the most after this move was that my mom continued to be physically abusive. On my thirteenth birthday, she saw me in the hallway and punched me hard in the arm because one of my friends had arrived at my birthday party early. For the first time, I punched my mother back. "Never punch me again," I yelled. "I'm not your personal beating bag!" That was the first time I stood up to her.

Sometimes I called my mom a brainwasher. She tried to fill my head with horrible ideas about my dad. She would order me to call him and say that I refused to go to his house for my regular bi-monthly visit. I cannot remember how old I was, but the one time I did this, my dad was so angry he came into my mother's house looking for me. Before he got to the door, my mom told me to hide in my bedroom, promising that she would not let him in. She lied. Not only did he come in, but he started yelling at me about how I had hurt him for refusing to visit on a weekend when his family was there. It was sickening that my mother did nothing but watch with a half smirk on her face. She appeared not only to have some level of satisfaction in what she saw, but she actually enjoyed it. I did go with dad and then tried desperately to stay, but I had to return to my mom's house. Begrudgingly.

During the years when I lived with my mom, I never felt safe. I always felt powerless to get out of my situation. My response was to isolate myself, lying to avoid punishment, and creating imaginary realities that were safe. After a while, I started hearing my siblings talk about my peculiar behavior.

Not only did my mother abuse me psychologically and physically, but also my stepdad began touching me inappropriately. The first time was shortly after my mom asked him to stay overnight with her. I was seven-years-old.

The man would kneel on the floor and start tickling me. The first time I thought maybe he meant to grab my inner thigh and missed, but his probing touch happened every time he played that game. I told him I didn't like what he was doing, but he continued. And then he took his games to the next level. He got really fond of playing on the floor on all fours, like a hungry animal hunting his prey. Then he came to attack me, snorting and chomping his jaws like a rabid beast. It always ended with my wrists pinned together in one of his hands. He held my hands over my head and positioned himself on top of me, whether on my back or stomach. Once I was immobilized that way, he used his free hand and face to attack me.

During the winters, on very cold nights, the skin on my back would get dry enough to crack, leaving me with sore spots. My mom would ask the man to put lotion on my back. He had me lie facedown on my mother's bed, and then he would push my shirt all the way up over my shoulders. While he applied the lotion, I always felt his hands creep between my arms and my side then down to the front. I started squeezing my arms tight against my sides to stop him from doing that, in case it was an accident. In this way, I convinced myself, I would let him know he was not in the right place. But my efforts were futile. He never stopped. He just pushed harder to move his hands where he wanted them to go.

From early elementary school into early high school, these scenarios played out multiple times a week. The difference was the elements involved and the duration. It became normal for me to expect it. I believe that during my middle school years, I started compartmentalizing myself. I did not develop a split personality, but I intentionally separated aspects of my life, to help me survive the abuse mentally and emotionally.

I tried to ignore the abuse and I created positive alternatives in my mind while the actual scenario was playing out. This was something like holding my breath through the bad things that happened to me, the things I had no control over. For positive life moments, my response was excessive, far beyond what an event warranted. It was like getting a candy bar and responding as if I had won a million dollars. Little did I know the kind of a personality that I was creating for myself. I feel as if I am only just now, in my forties, resolving who I was with the woman I have become. I actively work at making peace within myself by first addressing forgiveness. I have worked—and continue to work—hard to learn better and more genuine ways of responding to life storms.

During the summer 1988, after I completed my freshman year of high school, I was in the attic going through my boxes when my stepfather joined me. On that note, it was time for me to leave. I positioned myself to start my ascent down the ladder when he grabbed me in a completely inappropriate location. "Don't touch me there again," I shouted at him.

"What? I was just trying to keep you from falling," he chuckled.

I snapped back, "I was not even on the ladder yet."

As soon as I could, I rushed to the phone and pleaded with my dad to come get me right away. "Please," I begged. "I can't live here anymore. I need you to get me." I told him I'd be waiting at the end of the driveway. "I'm on the way," Dad said.

I packed a few clothes, stuffed animals, and special trinkets from friends, enough to fill two medium-sized cardboard boxes, and carried them to the end of my driveway. On the way out the door the last time, I turned to my mother and told her, "If you'd put out more for your husband, he wouldn't think he had to get it from me." I did not listen for a response as I walked to the driveway. I sat on the boxes and waited for my father to arrive.

While I waited for my dad to make his thirty-minute drive, I berated myself about how I allowed myself to become a damaged human by not escaping sooner. Then my mom came outside, crying hysterically and begging me to come back into the house. She told me that she would call my dad and tell him not to come and she would help me unpack. Without looking at her, I sharply stated, "My things are packed. These boxes will never be unpacked until they're in a new home." In time, she gave up and went inside before my dad arrived. Then I started visualizing freedom. It was as if I had been captive and suppressed, confined to a bubble for all those years. I seemed to watch myself climb out of the bubble as I took my first true breath of air. I knew everything was going to get better then.

That same summer, my sister moved into her own apartment and my brother stopped his regular visitations with our dad. The only part I regret was that I left without saying good-bye to my friends or my siblings. I walked out and did not turn back. Fortunately, in recent years, several of those middle school friends have found me on Facebook.

Because I left without saying goodbye or telling my brother and sister what happened, my mother could lie to them about why I left and what happened. For years, I didn't know what she said, but I knew it was bad enough for my brother to stop talking to me. Finally, to my great relief, we spoke on the phone shortly before my first marriage, and he told me what our mother had said to him. All terrible lies. Unfortunately, since I didn't know how to prove my innocence to my brother, our relationship remained strained for several more years.

The first night at my dad's house, I explained to my father and his third wife, Sherry, all that had happened to me and why I called for help. I told them that I had reached out several times, but no adult intervened to stop the abuse—no neighbors, clergy, or teachers. After our talk, my dad didn't take any actions against my mother or stepfather, to my knowledge. However, he told me that he called my mom and threatened action if it ever happened again. My dad also promised that I would never again have to return to my mom's house. However, that promise did not stop her from calling his house to speak with me. Or, more accurately, to torment me. She called to accuse me of a whole host of sins, using awful language. She charged me with sleeping around and said I would never amount to anything. Those messages swirled around in my mind, haunting me. Many times, I hung up on her and immediately informed my dad, so he could deal with the situation.

During all the years while I lived with my mother, so many people said horrible things to and about me, that I started to believe what they were saying. I withdrew from everyone, almost to the point of becoming a recluse. Whenever things were not going well, I felt as if someone pushed a button on my back and instantly those horrible statements would begin to replay in my head. Over and over again. I started believing the lies, so I withdrew from the world and turned myself inward, attempting to become invisible. I felt filthy, not worthy of being near anyone, and completely deserving of what harm came to me. My futile attempts to escape those lies found me creating false realities to comfort myself. I lived in a made-up fantasy world. Not only was this process tiring, but this fantasy identity made me feel as if I was not a real person. That way of living lasted through most of my young life.

Fortunately, when I moved in with my dad, I realized I desperately needed to stop believing those lies. Much like *Sleeping Beauty*, it was time to wake up and start living life. At last, I was in a safe place to make that happen. Even before I realized it, I knew something was protecting me. Definitely, when I look back now, I see it. My survivor's heart was receptive to a spiritual being long before I knew what to call it. This mental strength allowed me to fight for survival and immense faith. That's how I walked with baby steps out of the oppression at my mom's house.

During the fall of 1988, I started my sophomore year in high school at a performing theater arts school, Broad Ripple High, in Broad Ripple, Indiana. No one there knew me, so I realized I could become anyone I wanted to become. During the summer before this term, my dad paid for modeling classes, which did wonders for my self-confidence, while reducing my shyness. The first day of school, I decided I needed to smile at everyone and start with "Hello". That day I was amazed to learn how successful a smile and hello could be for me. I made several friends before I went home.

During this year, I joined the track and field team, and discovered a great interest in drawing and acting. There are no words to describe the feeling I had while being able to explore my desires and abilities. In addition to identifying recreational interests, I realized that I loved school. My academics started to soar. Teachers enrolled me in advanced placement classes. These experiences taught me the extent of my mom's oppression.

My sophomore year got even better. I met Cristi Clock. She was in the eleventh grade, skinny, and much taller than I was. She had the most beautiful long, extra-curly, bouncy, blond hair. In my eyes, she looked like *Alice in Wonderland*. We met in Mrs. Merchant's geometry class. This teacher had a reputation for being very mean, so students tried to avoid being placed in her class. We told each other that she was out to flunk us, although I actually started to like Mrs. Merchant by the end of the term because she challenged me. Cristi and I struggled together through this class and, thankfully, came out on the other side with passing grades. The best part of the course was my introduction to Cristi.

It was wonderful to move in with my dad. However, he had too many demands on his time, inside and outside our house. He was the chaplain at Methodist Hospital and he owned a family counseling practice. When I saw him, it was usually late at night, after he returned home and I had completed my homework. Every once in a while, he prepared a pot of Campbell's tomato soup and grilled cheese sandwiches cut into finger-like slices. He made enough for the two of us to share and we took that time to catch up. Those are among my favorite memories. I still get misty-eyed when I think about our very special connections.

Unfortunately, those nights did not happen often enough. While I had escaped the oppression and abuse I suffered under my mom's roof, I did not feel I was getting enough direction and attention from my dad. This is when I started looking outward. Fortunately, several teachers figured out that I needed personal guiding attention. They gave me extra time outside of class to offer advice and direction. I also had the added benefit of my friends' parents, specifically, Cristi's parents.

I was so fortunate that Cristi came from a fantastic family— which became more important to me over time, as I began to model myself after them. They were never judgmental and always full of love and guidance. However, there were times that I chose not go to them because I thought I might disappoint them. Regardless, I knew that when I absolutely needed them, they would be there. They let me come around often enough that I began referring to them as Momma and Papa Clock.

Okay, okay, now we come to the night that changed my life. Cristi's bedroom resembled a loft. The stairwell was on the left side of the room, with a railing across the top. As soon as we reached the top step, we faced a window. With a right turn, we faced another window. The fourth wall equally divided the top floor and had a door leading into her older sister's room. The ceiling was attic style, sloped on two sides. Cristi's bed was in a little nook outside her sister's room.

That night, I was lying on the floor next to her bed, staring at the light streaming in. It reverberated around the arched ceiling. Sparkles of light glistened on the ceiling above me. The room seemed magical to me, and I basked in the peace and comfort. I started wishing this were my home.

Then, just as I was drifting off to sleep, Cristi whispered, "Have you invited Christ into your heart?" With a sluggish voice, I replied, "I don't think so, but I don't know. How would I know?" All my life I believed that to ask Christ into my heart would involve many bells and whistles and include elaborate rituals. She laughed softly. "Talking to Jesus is no different from the two of us talking, Gretchen."

I was confused and wondered how I could "just talk" to someone I couldn't see. "Why don't you talk to your pillow?" she suggested. "That will give you something to look at, and Jesus won't mind."

That night, in June 1989, I spoke from my heart. "Lord Jesus, I love you very much, and I'm asking that you please come live in my heart forever and always. Please change my heart to be in alignment with yours."

I did not feel instantly transformed, but I did recognize change beginning to develop within me.

Cristi's family became an intricate part of my personal fabric. As the years passed, we discovered that it didn't matter how much time spread out between our conversations. Every time we did talk, it was as if we hadn't skipped a beat. In fact, on August 30, 2014, Papa Clock drove Cristi and her eleven-year-old daughter several hours in each direction so they could attend my dad's "celebration of life" after he passed away. There Papa Clock reminded me that he could never replace my daddy, but that if I ever needed a father to call on, he was available to me. This extension of my own family is an example of a very special and recurring silver lining in my life.

In January of 2016, I had to say goodbye for now to Papa Clock. I am fortunate to have two daddy angels looking over me.

# Chapter 2
# My Source of Strength

About a month after my transformational night at Cristi's house, in July 1989, she invited me go with her on a babysitting job. The home where we were going was about seven miles from my dad's house, in a ritzy condominium complex. "Sure," I said. "Why not? Afterwards, we can find a place to eat."

I quickly discovered that hunger would become my least important concern that night. After the child's mother left, I started having a dull ache in my right side. The pressure felt as if someone was tightly squeezing me simultaneously from the front and back. While the pain wasn't persistent, it was strong enough to acknowledge. In an attempt to minimize the discomfort, I redirected my attention to entertaining the little girl. We played with dolls and puzzles while watching television. Those activities proved successful at helping me forget about the pain.

The child's mother arrived home long after any restaurant's closing hours, which defeated our dining plans. Regardless, Cristi and I still wanted to do something—anything but go straight home. We came up with this wild idea to decline the ride home so we could enjoy the adventure of a walk instead.

The start of the walk was fantastic. It seemed as if time was endless and we could go anywhere we wanted. We talked about everything that came to mind. Mostly boys.

On our journey, we felt safe walking on the shoulder of the four-lane road lined with a wall of trees. Unfortunately, the farther we walked, the darker the night became. At one point, the night grew so dark that we could no longer see our feet below us. Just as the darkness descended, the pain in my side recurred with an intensity that seemed to push my tolerance threshold to its outer limit. The situation was further complicated when we realized that we were much farther from my house than we originally thought. Instantly we recognized how vulnerable we were, and fear swept over us. Our minds began creating potential dangers.

We thought about who might be sleeping in the woods and who might abduct us. Where were these thoughts before we started walking? The minimal lighting on the very straight road made us feel, at times, as if the road was actually growing longer or, at best, that we were walking in place. Fortunately, neither of these were reality.

About a mile from my house, one of our friends drove past us and then turned around to pick us up. Though my pain was intense, I didn't mind stuffing myself into the tiny back seat; it was a welcome relief from walking.

At Dad's house, my bedroom was in the basement. My dad, step-mom, and younger brother all slept on the second floor. That night, my body hurt so much that all I could think about was their distance from me. I could not stand the thought of making any move of my aching body to reach them. I spent hours trying to fall asleep, but the pain prevented any rest. However, I must have fallen asleep at some point because I remember waking up in even more excruciating pain. It was constant and sharp, like an ice pick repetitively darting deeply into and out of my flesh, each time stabbing a slightly different location. I felt so hot that it seemed a raging inferno had rendered me mindless.

In an attempt to process my options, I knew that I needed help, and I had to climb out of my bed to get it. No matter how slow or careful I was with my movements, the pain dramatically intensified. As I slid out of my bed, my head was pounding, my stomach was nauseous, and my legs felt as rubbery as cooked spaghetti. I scooted across the floor to the bottom of the first stairway. When I looked up, I saw what appeared to be an ever-lengthening tunnel. I felt helpless at the prospect of climbing. However, I knew I had to "just-do-it!"

Tears rolled down my cheeks as I attempted to yell, "Help me." But no one responded, so I began a shaky ascent up the stairs. Each step was excruciating as I braced my right mid-section with my left hand. I took a deep breath and pulled hard with my right hand on the step above me while simultaneously pushing hard with my left foot on the step below me. Every move saturated my entire core with intense pain. I began to wonder where this God was that I had just asked into my heart. Why would he let me suffer like this? Still, even though I could not see him, I sensed a strong spiritual presence.

I tried again to yell for help when I reached the top step, but no one responded. After scooting through the kitchen, dining room, and family room on my butt, I approached the next set of stairs. Looking up that staircase, I didn't think I had the energy to complete the last leg of this journey, but I knew I had to try. I stopped on every step and gasped as much air into my lungs as I could before whimpering for help. Under my breath, I repeated, "Help me… Please, God, help me. You are supposed to be my help. Where are you? Please let someone hear me."

Time seemed to freeze in place as I eased up the stairs.

Finally, outside my dad's bedroom door, I continued to plead for help. "My God, I hurt so badly! Will someone please help me?" There are no words to describe the relief I felt when Dad finally came to the door. He carried me down the stairs, sat me on the couch, looked me over, and gave me some pain medicine. He asked me to hold out a few more hours until the doctor's office opened, to save me the pain of waiting in an emergency room.

For the next few hours, I tried to focus on whatever I could to keep my mind off the pain. Finally, we were in the car and Dad was driving to the doctor's office. In the examination room, the pains radiated down my entire right side and I found myself sweating profusely, even though I felt like I was in an ice bath. When they took my temperature, it was already over 104 degrees Fahrenheit. As soon as the doctor completed her examination, she instructed us to go to the emergency room, where help would be waiting for me.

By the time we reached the hospital, the pain was so intense that I felt as if my head was going to blow off and my body was going to split in half.

At the hospital, while waiting on the gurney for lab results, I did little more than sob from the pain. I was petrified. My dad sat next to me and put his hand on my head. "Honey, you look very scared," he whispered. "I am," I gasped. Looking back now, I believe he must have been praying for me when he touched my head because even feeling that degree of pain, I felt a moment of peace.

An hour later, the medical staff quickly prepared me for emergency surgery, telling us they believed that my appendix was about to rupture. Events unraveled so quickly that, other than intense pain, I only vaguely remember what took place between arriving at the emergency room and becoming alert in the recovery room after surgery.

Waking up, I felt a sense of relief and hope that they had resolved my issue. When the orderly wheeled me to my regular hospital room, my first guest was already waiting for me. It was my twin brother, Jon. I saw him sitting on the window ledge, and I noticed behind him that the sun was starting to go down. "Has an entire day already gone by?" I asked myself. However, time didn't really matter. I was going to get better now. And my brother had come to see me.

This was the first moment I actually considered the passage of time and the comings and goings of people taking care of me. I was excited to greet each visitor who entered my room—until later in the evening, when my stepmom's sister and her family came to visit me. I could not hold my eyes open, no matter how hard I tried. I apologized for being a horrible host because I really wanted to talk to them. I thought about how far they had driven to visit and I didn't want to disappoint them, but I just could not keep my eyes open.

Shortly after the last visitors left my room, my nurse returned with the thermometer. This time while she was taking my temperature, I had to force my eyes to focus. Each time they opened, I saw my temperature going up. First, 102…Then, 103…104…105…106. "I think your thermometer is broken," I told the nurse.

"No, it's not," she said with concern on her face. I remember thinking how calm she was, especially when I thought I should be dead with a temperature like that. I realized my only option was to surrender my life. Maybe, I told myself, this was my time to go.

I rolled my head back onto the pillow, looked at the ceiling, and closed my eyes. Then I said to myself, "Okay, God, here I am, if you're ready for me."

As soon as I shut my eyes, I heard several doctors and nurses scurrying around like ants on a mound. I opened my eyes and recognized every one of them. Who was the patient? I wondered. "Wait! It's me!" I marveled. I was watching them work on me. But…what was going on?

I could see my own face. In addition, I could see my body, but from some spot outside and above my body. Really? Somehow, I was hovering near the ceiling, looking down on this scene. How could that possibly be? I asked myself.

The doctors and nurses were placing zip-lock bags filled with whole ice cubes on my groin, armpits, and other areas around my body. They had taken my blanket and sheet off and were working hard to cool me down—quickly. Yet not too fast. After a couple minutes of watching, I felt myself falling toward the bed, where I returned to my body.

That was not the end of travel outside of my body, however. As soon as I dropped back into my body, I felt myself catapulted forward into a tunnel where there was no color. Everything was gray. A light brighter than the sun was at the far end of the tunnel, and I was moving toward it.

As I progressed into the tunnel, I felt a deep peace. No human words can begin to explain the sensation of lightness. I didn't know where I was, but I knew I didn't feel fear or pain. The question of my mortality crossed my mind, probably more so from curiosity about my destination, how long I would be there, and what my existence was about to look like. For certain, I knew that I had absolutely no control over my current situation. As I continued the journey into the tunnel at a pace slower than a snail, white misty figures flew past me, whizzing by so fast that I could not determine what they were.

Then, one at a time, random individuals came into focus. They were people from my past who had died before me. No matter who they were, they all came to me with a HUGE smile and words of encouragement. What struck me as odd was that their mouths did not move when they talked. Instead, their mouths only created smiles. Yet, I heard each one speak to me.

One said, "God does not think you're a bad girl. Neither should you. Stop being so hard on yourself."

The next one said, "You are doing GREAT. God is proud of you."

Another said, "You are going to live many years, to a ripe old age, and you'll reach more people than you could ever imagine."

The last one confirmed the fact that I was not drawing any closer to the light at the end, when it told me, "It's not your time, so you have to go back."

I never made it farther than one-third of the way down the tunnel, but I distinctly recall how amazingly comfortable I felt. So much genuine love seemed to envelop me, and I wanted more. I loved hearing from the people of my past, even though I could not really talk to them. That conversation was one-sided. It felt immensely comforting to know that they, and especially my spiritual head, were proud of me.

I never saw the descent back into my body – I just found myself back on the hospital bed. When I opened my eyes, I was lying in my room, and a nurse was standing next to me. I thought I had only been sleeping for a couple of minutes, until I noticed that it was daylight outside the window. Everything felt so different, and I could not figure out why. My eyes studied the room in the same way a curious newborn baby might.

To my left, I noticed my roommate was no longer there. I asked where she was. "She's been discharged," the nurse told me. Later, I learned that the nurses had moved her to another room because of what was happening with me. A young girl would be terrified to have a roommate in dire distress, let alone to watch a death take place in a shared room.

The nurse started asking me questions to determine if I was alert: "What is your name?" she asked, followed by, "What day is it?" and "Who is the president?" After she finished her series of questions, I continued observing new things. There was a large machine at the end of the bed attached to a thick mat under me. The mat covered the entire bed. I remember thinking that they had to move me to place it there. I am a light sleeper, and a move like that would certainly have awakened me. Could that move have been the reason for the jolt I felt right before I catapulted into the tunnel?

I felt confused, overwhelmed by all the details I vaguely recalled. I began working to put the pieces of this puzzle together. I asked the nurse if anyone had come into the room while I was "asleep". She said that she hadn't heard of anyone stopping by, but she would check. Apparently, since I was a minor, the medical staff was supposed to document all of my visitors, including parents.

"No, no one is in the log book," the nurse informed me when she returned. I believe the significance of "no visitors" was that I had recently asked God into my heart. I needed to trust that I was taken care of by Him. Besides, I really did have a sense of peace knowing my spiritual head was with me the entire time. This may be exactly what I needed to see: that I am never alone.

After two weeks in the hospital, I could not wait to go home. What made my homecoming even better was having an awesome friend like Cristi. Unfortunately, while I was in the hospital, she had decided to take a mini road trip with another friend to a party at Indiana

University and didn't tell her parents. This resulted in a very steep punishment. Her parents restricted her activities to school, work, and home. She could go nowhere else. Regardless, she risked deeper consequences by coming to visit me.

Cristi was eager to see how I was feeling, since the last time we had seen each other was the long and excruciating walk home just before my trip to the hospital. This was one time where I fully endorsed her defiant actions—besides, she brought ice cream. This visit instantly sent healing endorphins throughout my veins and zapped my energy into overdrive.

Even with less than an hour to visit, we managed to catch up on everything that took place during our two weeks apart. Cristi was a silver lining for this life walk.

I was home for less than twenty-four hours before my temperature spiked above 104. Back to the hospital I went. This time I wasn't suffering the same kind of pain I had felt two weeks prior, but I wondered whether my fever would ever go away.

Upon re-admittance, doctors determined that I was suffering from a serious kidney infection. They speculated that this same infection was what caused my severe temperature that night after surgery. The extremely high temperature was an indicator that sepsis was in my body; the infection had permeated into my bloodstream. Fortunately, during this second admittance, doctors were able to identify the correct intravenous medication to annihilate the kidney infection and prevent further sepsis.

Only days after starting the new medication, I regained levels of energy that I had nearly forgotten were possible. Patients in the hospital in the 1980's had little to do but watch television, work on puzzles, and look at magazines. Boredom took hold of me—but fear not, I got creative and found my own entertainment.

I started playing with the bed's remote controls until I found myself stuck. To add to the humor of the situation, the bed's controller dropped on the floor, out of reach. I could not contain my laughter, which is what lured the nurse to my room. When she arrived at the door, she found me squished between the headboard and footboard of my bed. They were as vertical as I could get them, which was possible in 1980's hospital beds. She attempted to chastise me, but couldn't control her own laughter. I quickly discovered that she had a plan.

A patient who was just as bored as I was occupied a room on the other side of the nurses' station. My nurse decided we could help each other and it would be good to connect us for morale purposes. I am glad she did. Having someone my age to talk to made my time in the hospital go by much faster. One of our favorite things to do was to walk around the nurses' station and joke with them. If not for all the medical stuff—needles, medicines, vital signs, and various apparatuses—we would have felt we were in something resembling summer camp.

After receiving intravenous medication for several days, I showed significant improvement. To make things better, knowing my stepmom was a pediatrician, my doctor let me go home early. The one condition of my discharge was that I had to come back every day for a few hours to receive intravenous medication until the end of my treatment. My discharge day was bittersweet. I was allowed to go home, but my new friend had to stay.

Fortunately, we visited every day while I received my medication. To make things interesting, I pretended to smuggle his favorite snack items and magazines into his room. However, I had to be careful because he had diabetes. I hope that somehow during those days, I became a silver lining for him.

About a month later, that boy and I met at the Indianapolis State Fair for the first time since we both left the hospital. I don't remember much of what we talked about, but I do remember sharing my experience in the tunnel and the messages I received. He thought that was amazing.

Since the tunnel encounter after surgery, I frequently think back to the words that were told to me. Every once in a while, I wonder if I'm staying on the right track. Regardless, I believe with all my heart in the fulfillment of the statements spoken to me in that near-death experience. In fact, throughout this book, you will see multiple trials where I reflect back on the tunnel experience. I use it as a faith thermometer and a source of motivation and hope.

# Chapter 3
# Early Personal Development

When I look back on how I became the woman I see in the mirror today, I clearly recognize the driving forces behind both my positive and negative choices. Many of the self-destructive choices I made during my teen and young adult years stemmed from the circumstances in my early childhood. The first such circumstance occurred when my parents divorced. That was during the summer of 1980, when I turned seven. What compounded the situation was my mother's negative and terrifying responses to me.

The first night we were settled in our new apartment in Indianapolis, my mother sat down with my brother, sister, and me and confronted us with the question: "Who do you want to live with?"

After much debate with her about wanting to live with both of my parents, I announced that if I had to make a decision right then, I wanted to live with my dad. She retorted, "Well you can't. You have to stay with me because the judge said so."

I remember asking myself why, if she already knew that, did she ask. Unfortunately, I believe my answer directly influenced my mother's attitude toward me and led to the further deterioration of our relationship. While many years later, as an adult, I asked her to forgive anything I did to hurt her, and I have forgiven her for the many hurts she caused me, we rarely contact each other now.

The day my dad died, August 28, 2014, was the last day I called her. Even though I was clearly distraught on the phone, she remained emotionless and even redirected the conversation to talk about her husband. I was on the call less than three minutes before I hung up on her because of that insensitive response.

I believe it is in the best interest of my physical, mental, and spiritual health to move on through life without forcing interactions with my mother. I understand that my mother had a challenging youth; she lost both of her parents at a young age. However, regardless, I refuse to accept that as a viable reason for her brutal treatment of my siblings and me. No child deserves the abuse we endured.

Countless efforts to create a positive relationship with her have proven futile and caused me too much emotional and physical pain. These days I feel it is pointless and self-destructive to continue pursuing a relationship with her. However, she is my mother and I came into this world through her. For that reason, I respect her, love her, and make sure she is taken care of. Those things will never change. Of course, when she initiates contact with me, I will not turn her away.

To my surprise, for whatever reason, during the past year she has contacted me three times. I'm not sure what initiated the sudden change in her desire to interact with me; perhaps it signals the beginning stages of dementia. Or the resurgence of a conscience. Those three calls collectively match the total number of her calls to me during the previous fifteen years. I don't really know how I feel about this, but for now I will take the time to talk to her.

I made too many negative choices in the early years after my parents divorced. I became very depressed and did not feel that I belonged anywhere. To deal with my extreme loneliness and fears, I created false realities for myself—to the point where I could not keep my lies straight. I remember crying often and hating my life always. The emotional oppression, physical abuse, and fears prevented me from functioning well. I wanted to kill myself.

One of my many attempts at suicide took place while I was in third grade. I climbed out of my second-story window and stood on what I thought was a wooden ledge; it was actually a drain for water. I tried to fall so that I would land on my head. This time, as well as several other times, I managed to twist at the last moment before hitting the ground. The worst injury I incurred was a bruised rear end.

The multiple attempts to drown myself were just a waste of time. The worst thing that happened was when I could feel myself inhaling water and the warmth of the water filled my nose and started traveling down my throat, I immediately forced myself out of the water. I draped myself over the edge of the bathtub like a limp rag. Then I let my head dangle near the ground as I coughed and choked the water out of my throat and lungs.

Finally, after multiple failed attempts to escape from my mother's house permanently, I successfully moved out of her house and into my father's house during the summer of 1988, following my first year in high school. I could begin a new life with my dad and stepmother. I still have medical records that illustrate my unhealthy physical condition. At the age of fifteen, I weighed only eighty-three pounds and stood five feet one-and-one-half inches in height. I had been so depressed living with my mother that I lost any desire to eat, and when I did eat, I had issues with an upset stomach. I vomited often. Living in my dad's house, where I was loved and cared for, made a huge difference in my life. By the end of the first year in my new home, I had put on thirty-three pounds, making me a healthy one-hundred-sixteen pounds.

I felt free, as if I had just accepted a second chance at life. I even came out of my shell enough to start modeling, acting, and running track. However, even with the positive life changes, many deep psychological scars remained from the years of oppression and abuse. I wanted to be near people and do what I could to make them happy because it felt good to be with people who wanted to be with me.

This led to more bad decisions. I found myself doing whatever I needed to get people [more specifically, men] to like me. I became a people pleaser, which led to a promiscuous phase in my life. It felt good when young men showered me with compliments and the touches that I grew up believing were synonymous with love.

I wanted to do what would make them happy, so they would shower me with more compliments. That would feed my poor self-esteem and make me feel wanted and loved, I told myself. More nights than I care to remember or mention, I snuck out of the house to have sex. I left from the basement door at or around midnight and walked around the block to where a male friend of mine would be waiting for me. We would drive to another location, have sex, and then I would return home before the people in my house woke up.

I never enjoyed the act. I always wanted it to be over as quickly as possible. Some nights after I returned home, I would cry because I felt so dirty. For the first year and a half, there were no walls around my bedroom; it was just the open basement. The clothes washer and dryer, sump pump, and wash sink lined the back wall, to the right side of my room. On the extra-emotional nights after sex, I used the sink like a shower to clean myself. However, it didn't matter how much I washed, it was not possible to wipe away the filth that seemed to cover me, inside and out. Yet I reminded myself that I just wanted to be loved. That was the only way I knew how to attain it.

Do you remember my near-death experience at the hospital? A kidney infection caused all those symptoms. What I didn't tell you was how I got the kidney infection. My promiscuity caused it. I didn't know that I needed to go to the bathroom after sex to flush out the bacteria. Evidently, one time when I didn't, the potentially fatal infection developed.

Nevertheless, my promiscuity resulted in much more serious consequences than a kidney infection. Before I graduated from high school, I had gotten pregnant twice and miscarried both times. I believe these self-destructive, desperate times is why Cristi came into my life. She became the silver lining that helped me identify my source of faith and hope.

By the time I turned twenty, I felt as if I had stabilized my life. I had a strong faith, a good job, and I had returned to college. I stopped my promiscuous behaviors and found myself in a serious relationship with the first person who, I believed, genuinely cared about me for more than just sex. We spent more time just hanging out talking, watching television, and dancing than engaging in intercourse. Within several months of dating, we became engaged. Then, after less than a year, my newfound stability proved fragile. Once again, my life quickly fell apart, and chaos crashed in around me. This happened when my fiancé broke off our engagement.

About four weeks after that relationship ended, Cristi saw how depressed I had become and decided she needed to help me reengage in a life with excitement and something to look forward to. One night we drove from Indianapolis to Chicago, to visit some of her friends there. Several hours after our arrival, we drove back home in the early hours of the morning. What is better than the freedom of an unplanned road trip with no obligation to be on time anywhere? The trip was exciting and liberating—until, that is, my vulnerable state and the influence of alcohol invited the former promiscuous habits to return. This led to a one-night stand before we returned to Indianapolis.

About a week after the trip, my ex-fiancé called to tell me that the navy was sending him to boot camp earlier than he had expected, and he wanted to see me before he left. Even though we were not currently in a relationship, the engagement had only recently ended. Of course, I wanted to see him.

After dinner, he asked if he could stay with me that night before he shipped out in the morning. A few weeks later, I realized I was in a distressing situation when my monthly cycle was late. I asked Cristi to take me to the pharmacy to buy a pregnancy test.

We drove back to her house before I took the test. I knew if the results were positive, I could talk to her parents. When we got to her home, I did the whole process I had done too many times before: pee on a stick and wait for results. Who would have thought that five minutes could pass that slowly? The tick-tock from the clock in the background seemed very slow, yet quite pronounced. I could hear each breath magnified in my head, audibly competing with my high-speed heart rate. I felt like I was holding my breath for the entire five minutes, and I wondered if the wait caused me to age multiple years.

Results were in. I was pregnant. Now I was terrified. Cristi asked if she should get her mom. I said yes, because I needed a strong maternal figure to let me know everything was going to be okay, and I trusted Cristi's mom.

When Momma Clock came into the room, she sat down next to me. Without a word, she embraced me. Then she asked, "What are you going to do?"

I told her there was only one thing I could do.

Even though this was not my first pregnancy, it was the first one I was certain would produce my first-born. I would keep the baby, and I would make myself become a strong, positive, loving mother. I dedicated myself to doing what was necessary to protect this pregnancy, and I tapped into my faith for strength to get me through this unexpected storm.

By this time, my family relationships were either shattered or strained. After moving in with my dad, I never had regular contact with my twin brother or older sister, thanks to our mother's interference. This left my siblings oblivious to the majority of my high school life after I moved out of our mother's home. Maybe it was because of our ages at the time, or perhaps we were so absorbed in our own survival modes, but we made no real effort to contact each other.

As for my dad and stepmother, Sherry, they were my lifesavers for letting me come live with them. However, their relationship was relatively new, less than five years old when I moved in, and they had just had a baby, my younger stepbrother. I felt as if my dad had started his life over with a new family. Yes, my siblings and I were still his children, but we were almost grown. The majority of his attention was devoted to his new family. I would not say I was an afterthought while I lived with Dad, but I would say that I felt like I was in their way and unintentionally causing conflict in their new life together.

Have you ever heard the statement, "You can't have two queen bees in the same beehive?" Well, that is what was taking place between my stepmom and me. It was her house, her man, and her baby until I came along. Sherry had never lived with a teenaged daughter before. Her only child at the time was a baby boy. It goes without saying that there is night and day difference between rearing a baby boy and guiding a teenaged girl who had just escaped from a disastrous previous life. Truth be told, the easiest to raise—by far—was the baby boy.

Tensions grew between Sherry, my dad, and me. Sherry wanted to maintain her matriarchal position in her own hive and I wanted to exert strength in my newfound freedom. I was testing the proverbial waters, and she was not happy about that. Remember, up to this point, I believed I was nothing and worthless. Now, I merely wanted to see the breadth of my wingspan, what my capabilities were in a "safe" place. Unfortunately, this was the fuel that ignited intense emotions.

My dad was a wonderful husband who wanted to do everything to protect his family and keep his wife happy. I'm sure you can see where I'm going with this. In his desire to keep her happy and protect his family, whenever I kicked the beehive, the wrath of the nest came swarming all over me. More times than I care to count, my father forced his face within an inch of my face. He was so close when raging fury spewed from his lips that I could almost taste food particulates from his dinner the night before. It was as if he had stingers on both sides of his tongue as he lashed his anger at me.

In my new life, I realized I had a stubborn side, and I used it to exercise my right to fight back. Our verbal arguments became so violent that many times I thought someone would call the police. Eventually this became old. I wanted a clean break from my entire family. I moved out of my dad's house just before I turned eighteen. I was finally my own person. Until, that is, I met my first husband. Our wedding was the last time we saw or talked to family for years, except for brief connections around some holidays and birthdays.

From the beginning, this pregnancy presented many challenges. Due to extreme stress from the difficult relationship with my ex-fiancé, I was again grossly underweight at the time of conception. The doctors did not think I could carry the baby to term. They diagnosed my pregnancy as high-risk. When my mom found out about my pregnancy, she did not believe it, so she came with me to one of my doctor appointments to see for herself. Later, I found out that she was telling people that I needed to go to a home for unwed mothers and put my child up for adoption. I did not see that as an option.

I was unable to work because of the risk, so I was in desperate need of assistance. My mom's brother and his wife allowed me to move in with them. They offered me a safe place to start getting things in order for my son.

First, I needed to contact both men about the pregnancy. I don't think I need to explain just how trashy I felt to be in this position. It was horrible, but I knew it was something I needed to deal with. While the act of having two sexual partners in one week did not earn me the scarlet letter, I feel like I wear the imprint regardless.

The one-night-stand guy immediately changed his phone number and avoided me at all costs. To this day, he has little to do with his son and refuses to tell his wife he has another child. Contacting my ex-fiancé was difficult because he was in boot camp. When I finally reached him, I told him there was a 50/50 chance the baby was not his. He chose not to talk to me for a while as he processed what he heard.

A couple weeks after our telephone conversation, he called and asked me to marry him. I knew I needed to do this to ensure the health and safety of the baby. And me.

Minutes before the wedding, I stood in front of the bathroom mirror, trying to give myself a pep talk. What came out was, "He's not the one for me. Now what do I do?"

I was confused and too young to know how to handle my situation. Like a little girl, I stood there and wished for a fairy godmother to remove the storm that I knew was brewing after my decision to wed. All the elements were right in front of me, screaming that this marriage was a bad idea: It was a shotgun wedding. My sister was my only attendant. Not one of my closest friends was present. I wasn't in love, and I didn't think the bridegroom was, either. My gut took a clip out of the movie *Lost in Space*, when it started shouting, "Danger! Danger, Will Robinson." The message was clear: I needed to get out of that place.

I closed my eyes and visualized Cristi walking into the bathroom, wrapping her arm around my shoulder, and ushering me out the back door. To this day, I will tell you, if someone had come in and told me it was okay to leave, that wedding would not have happened. The reality is that no one ever came to me while I stood in front of that mirror.

Instead, I took a deep breath, walked into the sanctuary, and proceeded with the union. The night did not offer confirmation of a good decision. Rather, I spent the entire honeymoon evening with my head over the toilet, vomiting. Was this a result of pregnancy nausea or nerves over what appeared to be a bad choice? The answer was probably a bit of both.

This wedding was the last time I saw my siblings for many years. Even to this day, conversation takes place through a meager handful of telephone connections per year or short two-line messages through Facebook and text.

The next day, we were on the road to my new husband's base assignment in Florida.

51

I was married and about to have my first child, TJ. I should have been a happy woman. However, it quickly became evident that my pre-wedding jitters had merit. My husband was an alcoholic who denied having a problem, which led him to abuse me. Most of the abuse was verbal, but there were some physical episodes, too. As for faith, he was an agnostic and let me know that he didn't like it when I attended church. He even attempted to control me by making me feel inferior and belittling me in public.

I was hundreds of miles away from home, dealing with a high-risk pregnancy, and living with a man who abused me. I was fortunate to cross paths with Rana Strabley and her husband Chris.

My new husband and I rented a small studio apartment in a building that resembled a motel. It had two levels and three sides that wrapped around a little pool. Rana was the resident manager. Her husband was in the military, one of my husband's peers. Rana and I were three-hundred-sixty-four days apart in age, and both of us were pregnant, with due dates only days apart. Together, we were a recipe for life-long friendship.

As arguments arose with my then-husband, or when he became drunk, Rana and Chris let me stay at their place so my husband couldn't hurt me. Then, when issues inevitably arose with the pregnancy, Rana was always the person who drove me to the hospital. She sat with me through all the testing and results. It was indescribably comforting to have her support and friendship in those dark early days of both marriage and pregnancy. Rana was my silver lining for this stage in my life walk.

After a year of marriage, my husband received orders to relocate to a new base. When I learned I would be moving away from Rana, my support line, I felt terribly alone. The year was 1995.

That was when my path crossed with a new friend, D'Arcy Greene.

At the new command, I met D'Arcy, who was also a military wife. Her husband and mine had the same rank. Finding this woman was exactly what I needed for this new walk in my life. My husband's agnosticism meant that he refused to allow me any faith system of my own. Regardless, I knew I needed to reestablish my faith, and D'Arcy helped me find my conduit. She introduced me to the church on base.

This new connection helped me recognize that I desperately needed to change my current living situation. I needed to get out from under this ongoing oppression, and my renewed faith offered the necessary strength and courage to embark on the next stage of my life: single parenthood.

I made an appointment with an attorney to begin the divorce proceedings.

The divorce was difficult because my husband refused to sign the documents. He continually said he didn't like one word or another in the property settlement. After about a year of arguing the small details, I finally went to his house and told him to point out all the words he didn't like. I changed them there, in front of him, so he would sign the papers. The divorce was finalized several months later, in February 1997.

While I was awaiting my divorce, I told myself the last thing I needed was to be in a relationship with another man. However, I must have needed a helpmate, because almost immediately a wonderful man named Chip crossed my path. Our meeting deserves a story all of its own, but for the sake of this book, I'll keep it short.

The story begins when the house where I lived with my toddler, TJ, was broken into. Afterwards, we left the place and stayed with a friend of mine. One day while I there, I answered her phone when it rang. At first, I thought I was talking to her dad, because the man had the same name. As it turns out, the Chip on the phone was a friend of hers. I was glad he was not her dad because I told her after the call that I thought her friend was a jerk. She remarked that it might have something to do with his desire to become an officer and fly airplanes [which, subsequently, he never did].

Later that same day, someone knocked at the door. When we opened the door, there Chip stood, as if he had jumped out of the movie *Top Gun* during the volleyball scene. He would be visiting with my friend and her family for the week before heading back to school.

That pretty much sealed my opinion that Chip was a jock and a jerk. I did not want anything to do with him, and I tried to avoid him by every means – until we paired up as a team during a card game. By the end of the night, we were talking as if we had known each other for years. Something about our conversation was powerful because it left me feeling as if he was *the* one, my forever silver lining.

Another year down the road found us married and expecting our daughter Ashley. This pregnancy also proved difficult. In fact, it looked worse than the high-risk pregnancy with my first-born. At seventeen-and-one-half weeks' gestation, I went into full-blown labor. In the emergency room, I cried and repeated, "I don't want to lose my baby…I don't want to lose my baby!" Out of nowhere, an unfamiliar African-American woman gently placed her hand on my shoulder and said, "The Lord is with you. Your baby is going to be okay. Trust that!"

Warmth washed over me at her words, and instantly I knew, without a doubt, that everything was going to be fine. Usually if a woman goes into preterm labor before twenty weeks' gestation, the doctors send her home to abort naturally. However, within minutes of my encounter with that woman, the emergency room staff went against protocol and admitted me to the labor and delivery floor.

That night, of the five doctors on duty on the labor and delivery ward, all but one wanted to send me home and let the baby abort naturally. The one doctor who wanted to stop my labor was the chief of staff. You can guess who won that vote: the chief of staff. Later he confessed that he didn't believe our baby girl would survive. However, something told him that he needed to attempt to stop my contractions.

Several months later, when I introduced him to my daughter, who was beautiful, alive, and healthy, he expressed delight and surprise at the fact that she survived. I believe something miraculous took place through the hands and the words of that woman. She was our quiet silver lining.

Times were not easy, but I knew that my faith was strong enough to sustain me. I wanted nothing more than to know I was finally making the right decisions in my life—for my new husband, for the children, and for myself. I know now that I should have reflected more often on my near-death experience, where I heard that I was in fact "doing the right stuff."

I learned the hard way that there was no better time to exercise this goal than amidst the major life changes Chip and I were about to encounter, among them, relocation and frightening medical issues.

# Chapter 4
# Early Signs of M.S.

When Ashley was fifteen months old, in December 1998, we received orders to our next command, in the Cornhusker State. At our new home in Nebraska, we made a point of attending church on a regular basis, at least once a week and sometimes twice. Chip started reading the "Left Behind" book series and soaked it in like a happy sponge in water. This was the most remarkable spiritual transformation I had ever seen in him as he grew in faith.

I believe the timing of our growth in faith correlated with the next trial that was brewing. It appeared my health was on the chopping block this time. Chip was away on deployment during the winter of 2000, when a large snowstorm parked on top of us. In his absence, I was on snow-shoveling duty. That was not a big deal, because I acquired many physical jobs when he was on duty. This time, however, I felt physical constraints. My hands refused to keep a grip on the shovel, my arms did not want to bend, my legs felt heavy, and my vision became blurry.

In my late teens, I was a certified nursing assistant (CNA) while working toward obtaining my Licensed Practical Nursing (LPN) certification. During that time, I gained significant experience with neurological issues. This medical knowledge made it possible for me to recognize my symptoms as neurologic. Since both my mother and her brother have multiple sclerosis[1] (MS), I started questioning whether I might also have it.

I certainly didn't want MS, of course, so I tried to dispute my self-diagnosis, reminding myself that cooler weather was supposed to be better for MS. Yet I was finding it difficult to function during the winter months. Regardless, I worried about whether I was starting to develop MS, and I worried about what would happen if I had a major medical issue when Chip was deployed far way. After he returned home, we discussed our options and came to a mutual agreement that he would resign from active duty at the conclusion of his current orders.

In the fall of 2001, I completed my basic associate of arts degree at the local community college, which correlated with the end of Chip's orders. Friends and colleagues from the college came to help us pack our moving truck, and we left for Florida.

When we arrived in Florida, our temporary lodging was a single bedroom within the two-bedroom apartment that my sister-in-law and her husband rented.

In a storage unit near our temporary home, we stored all but a few essentials. We kept a queen-sized mattress for Chip and me, while both kids slept on the floor in sleeping bags. We kept some toys in the

---

[1] Information on Multiple Sclerosis Society is in Appendix B.

room for the kids and a television so they could watch children's shows. We used a small plastic storage shelf with drawers to hold toiletries, and our clothes were jammed into the small closet.

From the first day we arrived, Chip considered job-hunting to be his full-time job. Every day he looked for work. While he went on interviews and searched job ads, I took our seven-year-old son to school and entertained our three-year-old daughter. During the day, I completed simple housekeeping tasks as a way of thanking my in-laws for letting us stay with them. When the military pay ceased, we collected unemployment to make our financial ends meet.

In my family, I was the person who was responsible for paying the bills. Depression loomed over me as I watched the bills pile up. Then I began receiving a never-ending succession of calls from bill collectors. However, what broke my heart the deepest was watching Chip continually turned down for employment. I felt helpless as well as responsible for our situation. I feared the impact of the numerous unknown factors that collectively drove our decisions would swamp us.

In spite of how I felt, I knew I needed to hide my concerns and remain confident in Chip's abilities. I had to be strong for the family, especially with Ashley's fourth birthday right around the corner. It was already difficult trying to make that occasion a special day without adding my emotional stress to the mix.

Then things got worse.

A couple of weeks before Ashley's birthday, I felt odd things happening with my body. I could not walk in a straight line; rather, I oriented to the left. When I walked down a hallway, you could hear, step … thump … step … thump … step … thump. Once I took a step, what immediately followed was finding myself running into the wall like a mechanical toy missing a foot. I also noticed that when I grabbed for things with my left hand, I overshot whatever I was reaching for. Sometimes my strength was too much for the action I was performing. For example, when I lifted a tissue to my nose, I inadvertently punched myself in the face.

While these things were disconcerting, I made every effort to avoid going for medical care because we didn't have health insurance. Then came the night of the horrible headache. My head felt like a tube had been forced into my skull, a tube so full of pressure that I felt that it would pop at any time. I wondered if I was having a stroke. When I stood up, my left leg refused to hold my body weight. I realized the situation had become urgent. I needed to see a doctor immediately, even without insurance.

When we left for the hospital, Chip had to carry me to the car because I couldn't walk with only one functioning leg.

Going to the hospital without insurance was a tremendous hit to our already dwindling finances. With endless medical bills, no more military pay, and peanuts for unemployment assistance from the State of Florida, we were in a financial crisis. We realized the only way to get our heads above water was to file for bankruptcy. This significantly reduced stress on me at a time when I desperately needed to reduce stress in order to allow healing to take place.

As I waited in the Emergency Room, I wondered what was happening to me. Was it serious enough to take my life? I wondered.

Then I reflected on the message I had been given during my near-death experience years earlier. I'd been reassured that I would live to a very old age. Maybe old was relative to the age I had been when I heard those words? I debated silently. No, that was not possible, because I was now only in my mid-twenties. There was no way to misconstrue my age for old age, I told myself, trying to force a positive mindset.

While we waited for the doctor, I stayed as quiet as possible because my brain was working irrationally, asking and answering questions about my current condition. That appears to be something my mind likes to do during the hard times. I didn't want to share those irrational thoughts for fear I would further scare myself or spread the worries to Chip. However, I could not easily conceal my fears and anxieties. They were as thick in the room as pea soup, in spite of my efforts to remain quiet, optimistic, and as cheerful as possible.

Chip endlessly tried to calm me and lighten the mood by telling me jokes and funny stories. He even threatened to put me in the middle of the room so he could watch me walk in circles, chasing my own rear end. When his efforts at humor didn't work, he started playing with instruments around the room, until he came across the rubber glove dispenser. There he lingered for a few minutes, creating a rubber chicken that he sent to attack me as a rabid bird. Before long, I was giggling and laughing – quite a bit.

My mother-in-law, Ruth, worked at that hospital as a certified nurse's assistant. She knew I was there and wanted to check in to see how I was. When she walked into the room, she told me that she heard me laughing all the way down the hall. Ruth knew how petrified I was because she felt it too. However, she said she was concerned that the doctors might not take me seriously if they heard me laughing like that.

I was happy to see her and knew that she was sharing her concern, but I was glad that Chip helped me get my mind off the situation.

Shortly after Ruth arrived, the doctor came in and asked me the standard question: "What brings you in tonight?" I explained the symptoms, starting with my headache, then described how my left leg apparently grew a mind of its own and would not let me have a say in anything it did. During the exam, he asked me first to lift the non-affected right leg, an action that was quite uneventful. Then he asked me to lift the left one.

When I attempted to lift that leg, we all became spectators of something truly remarkable. The leg demonstrated clearly that it had a mind of its own, by kicking and flailing all over the air above me. The actions were so grandiose that the hospital gurney jerked around, almost bouncing off walls like a pinball game. The doctor ducked to avoid a blow from my foot and immediately instructed me to put my leg back down, but the leg had nothing to do with that request. The doctor had to grab my leg with both hands to push it down.

The doctor explained that the inability to control my leg was symptomatic of something neurological, and he sent me for a Computed Tomography (CT) scan of my brain. The scan revealed an abnormality in the center of my brain. After determining that I was not suffering an immediate life-threatening situation, he discharged me with a referral to a neurologist and an appointment the following day.

The next day we followed up with the neurologist on the referral. After reviewing my CT report, he brashly stated, "If the area of concern is a tumor, then it is inoperable due to the location." He appeared to be annoyed by my presence. I remember feeling terrified and angry. I wondered to myself why that doctor could not have more compassion for me. After all, I had not chosen to have problems in my brain. I had not asked for a malfunctioning body.

Consumed by fear and disgust, I walked out of that office—still wearing my hospital gown. I changed into my clothes in a bathroom just before the main exit of the office complex. After we left the building, I begged Chip to take me straight to a church. I was looking for a miracle. So many questions spun around in my mind. The answers never came, but I did find peace.

Maybe it was because this church was the first place where I found solace after all the medical hoopla. Maybe it was just a convenient location. Either way, we returned to that same church for Sunday service. Unfortunately, during that morning service, our experience was a total contrast from the prior visit. It was the most uncomfortable I have ever felt in a church.

I walked to the altar rail to receive communion and felt a deep peace, as if tightly embraced with loving arms. The feeling was so powerful that the floodgates to my heart opened wide, and I sobbed with an intensity that shook my soul.

In retrospect, I was shocked that no one spoke to me or asked me why I was crying so profusely, not even the pastor. Instead, they stared at me with questioning eyes. I felt as if they were inquiring about what I had done. They seemed to be asking silently what could be so bad that I needed communion to release my guilt and cause my tears. I told myself that their thoughts didn't matter. I knew I needed to be there because I could not move without my spiritual strength.

In the days that followed, I still had symptoms, but they became tolerable. I got used to walking in circles and not being able to button my own clothes or put toothpaste on my toothbrush. During this stage of the trial, vivid flashbacks flooded my mind. I focused on the connections I had made in my tunnel experience and the promise about living a long life. This silver lining was my deep faith.

I needed to establish my purpose for living and a way to accomplish it, because if I was going to be around for a very long time, I certainly did not want to live this way.

Initially I focused on regaining my physical abilities. To do this, we purchased a recumbent bike that I used multiple times a day to rebuild strength in my legs. For the upper body actions that caused me trouble, I worked to retrain those muscles by slowing down and focusing on properly completing each action.

About three weeks after my Emergency Room visit, on September 11, 2001, my phone was bombarded with calls from people asking if the military had called Chip back to active duty—six weeks after he had resigned. To the amazement of the friends on the other end of the phone, I didn't understand the purpose of their calls. Every one of them had been hysterical, shouting that one of the Twin Towers had been struck by an airplane and was falling down. "It's all over the news! How can you not know?" they asked.

Their sheer panic fueled my curiosity enough to find out what was happening. I rushed into another room and turned the television to CNN News minutes before the second airplane flew into the second tower. Wow! I had been dealing with major medical issues and Chip's unemployment, and now this. I cried and felt a strong urge to hold hands with strangers and pray. The nation seemed overwhelmed with so much confusion and feelings of hopelessness.

Days before the 9/11 catastrophe, we had received good news, however. Chip's endless efforts to look for work had paid off. He received a job offer for a government position at the Kennedy Space Center, and he gratefully accepted. Fortunately, for us, despite the national fears and concerns, the terrorist attack did not create a delay in his civilian employment. Chip started working a week later. The new job meant that it would be just a matter of time before we could have our own home, money to pay bills, and—most important of all—health insurance. While many of our difficult circumstances were being resolved, we still had unanswered questions and a feeling of uncertainty.

About two weeks after Chip started his new job, we found our new home and moved in. I still had neurological symptoms, but they didn't seem as bad as they had been. In fact, the remaining symptoms were not visible to others. That, we learned, is typical for this "invisible" disease, Multiple Sclerosis.

Now that we had insurance, I could go see a doctor who might be able to tell me what was wrong. The new doctor ordered a brain

Magnetic Resonance Image (MRI) to see if there were any changes from the hospital's Computed Tomography (CT) scan. He received the results on a Friday and called me into his office after closing time. "This cannot be a good thing," I told Chip. "It's never good when a doctor calls you into the office after hours."

The drive to his office was long, and it gave my mind ample time to fill in the blanks. Our minds can be horrible nuisances to us at times, as we try to make sense of a confusing or frightening reality.

When we arrived at his office, the doctor informed me that there was an area of concern identified in the middle of my brain. He added that there was not enough information to know without question if it was a mass. I recalled the words from the first neurologist, "If it's a tumor, it's inoperable." My surroundings blurred as a flood of tears fell into my lap. I thought to myself, "I'm only twenty-eight years old. I'm too young to die!"

Within minutes, however, I tuned in to the voices surrounding me. I focused on the conversation in time to hear the doctor say, "I'm sorry I can't give you more information than that." He spoke to Chip when he said, "Just watch her. She may start having mood swings. Depression could set in, or any number of psychological issues could surface."

"Lovely!" I thought. "As if these symptoms aren't bad enough, I have the potential to become a psychological nut case, too! What else is going to happen?"

I became very angry at my circumstances. When I got home, I felt as if I had to hold my breath for the entire weekend while I waited to see a new neurologist. My mind refused to focus on anything but the

MRI results, even though the report gave us very little information. The not-knowing part almost sucked the life right out of me.

Monday morning first thing found us sitting in another neurologist's office. I explained to the neurologist that both my mother and her brother have multiple sclerosis. He expressed his concern that I might also have it. Then more testing commenced.

In the coming weeks, I felt like a lab rat. I returned to the lab frequently for tests. There, technicians seemed to draw quarts of my blood at a time. I remembered asking them if it would be too much of an imposition to leave at least one drop of blood in my pipes. Twice, the sheer volume of blood drawn made me feel as if I was a blood donor times ten. Once, the lab technicians positioned me in a chair, leaned me back at a precipitous angle with my feet in the air, a beverage in one hand and a snack in the other so I wouldn't pass out.

Being stuck with needles and stuffed into machines multiple times a week grew old quickly. At the completion of all the testing, the doctor said that he believed I had MS, but he could not diagnose me yet because I had only one lesion, a scar on the brain. Months of testing concluded with, "Here's a box of information on Avonex. Read up on it and we will watch you for changes. If they occur, we can start you on the medication [Avonex]."

After all the invasive testing, I still had no answers to the question of why these crazy things were happening to my body—and if they would come back. I felt physically violated and drained. No longer did I desire to talk to anyone. I was broken and virtually told I could not be fixed. MS is a disease that doctors diagnose by ruling everything else out. They had effectively ruled everything else out, so why couldn't they work on fixing me now?

When all else had failed and there appeared to be no resolution or treatment for my ongoing symptoms, I reflected on the words spoken to me about living to be a ripe old age. Again, I decided I needed to find a way to live in spite of my circumstances. Remembering that people with MS could function better and have fewer symptoms in cooler, drier climates, I talked to Chip about moving us north. Unfortunately, I remembered this detail but failed to recall what the cold had done to me while we were in Nebraska. Regardless, another job search began.

# Chapter 5
# Persevering Through the Trials

In March of 2002, Chip started looking for work in the north. A company in Kentucky, Amazon.com, was the first to extend a job offer, and Chip accepted. For the first time in a year, our focus shifted off my health and onto a new, and what we hoped would be a promising, opportunity.

Time was no longer stagnant. Rather, it moved with a swift current. We spent every moment packing boxes and organizing items in preparation for the move to Kentucky. We put our house on the market, packed our moving truck, and headed northward toward a new start for all of us in late summer.

I only vaguely recall details of this move, other than the fact that we moved ourselves and stayed in temporary housing when we reached Kentucky. While we were house hunting, our relocation guide introduced us to a super-fantastic couple, Jack and Shirley, who took us under their wings. They loved on us so much. In spite of our bankruptcy from the previous year, they financed us to buy one of their investment houses. That was a silver lining in our lives.

After we settled in, I researched universities in close proximity and found one in town, a southern Baptist school called Campbellsville

University. I applied to the biology program and received acceptance within a few weeks.

Chip worked more than fifty hours a week during the off-peak season. During the peak seasons of Thanksgiving and Christmas, he oftentimes worked in excess of sixty to eighty hours a week. Because Chip worked so many hours, I often took the kids to school with me. One of my friends also had a school-aged child, so she and I interlaced participation with school functions for our children while diligently studying for our own coursework.

In the spring of 2004, I began my senior research Gretchen-style, attempting to defeat the odds when choosing my topic of choice in the field of biology. My plan was to complete an in-vitro fertilization of a rare species of fish. As I met with my academic advisors, they informed me that entirely too many unknown variables could prevent this research from coming through to fruition. Taking heed of what they said, I began a walk that would take six years to complete—full circle.

My research started in the field—or, more precisely, in the water—collecting my fish. When we gathered enough for my research, I brought them back to the lab. Once the fish fully matured, I stripped their eggs and milt solution (sperm) for in-vitro fertilization.

The fish were at the right stage for in-vitro fertilization just as Chip was deploying for his annual two-week commitment with the Navy Reserves. I packed our kids and brought them with me for the first day and a half of this research.

About a month later, I started noticing problems with my eyes. When they were open, I saw horizontal bands that rotated upward like an old television in need of a rabbit-ear adjustment. Worried that I would not be able to document developmental changes, I called my research advisor/mentor, Dr. Gordon Weddle, to check on the research specimen.

The first year's research results were limited, due to a copepod [parasite] infestation that killed my specimens. However, I obtained enough data to write my research paper. Dr. Weddle felt strongly enough about my research that he suggested I present the results at an annual undergraduate competition at Kentucky Academy of Science. He accompanied several students, including me, to the competition. There I earned second place for my research. "You did a good job and should be proud of yourself," Dr. Weddle told me. I felt a sense of pride to hear my mentor compliment my work. Along with the praises from several individuals came the suggestion to publish my research. That was a challenge I was ready to accept.

With all my successes, I fully believed that I had the ability to attain that goal. However, in order to get my research published, I needed more successful and thorough results. I planned to repeat the research in my final term at the university, during the spring of 2005.

The doctor prescribed steroids to resolve the situation with my eyes, and I found a neurologist who again investigated a possible MS diagnosis. Testing commenced, beginning with a nerve test, then more blood work, and another MRI. Everything was normal except the MRI, which now revealed more than one lesion on my brain.

I wanted a second opinion from a familiar face, my neurologist in Florida, so we decided to take an extended trip to Florida over the Christmas holiday. This way I could schedule an appointment with my old neurologist and have some time at the beach. I so missed the ocean, and I knew it would help me relax and melt away from reality, at least temporarily.

Sitting in the doctor's office, I felt nervous, but I believed he would confirm the diagnosis. One glance at my MRI was all he needed. "This is MS," he said unequivocally. Those words still ring in my head. He said it with such a matter-of-fact tone that it was as if I already knew—and, in reality, I did. I just didn't want it to be so. That night I cried, pleading for a miracle healing. I wanted nothing more for Christmas 2004 than for my diagnosis to be a mistake and for all the symptoms to go away.

Instead, we returned home, where I fell into a deep depression. I functioned like a pre-programed machine. Every day, I got out of bed, took care of my kids, attended my classes, and started MS treatment.

I chose a medication that I injected daily because it was supposed to have the fewest side effects. However, after the first few shots in January 2005, I started having injection-site reactions. The longer I took the medication, the worse my reactions became. The swollen areas were the diameter of a grapefruit and raised almost one-quarter inch in height. I injected the back of my arms, stomach, hips, and thighs. My body was only five-feet-two-inches tall and about 105 pounds. Between the large bumps and bruising, I started looking like a human-sized bumpy blackberry.

The pain became so fierce on all sides of my body that I could no longer sleep. During those sleepless nights, I often went into another room to cry so I wouldn't wake Chip. My body felt deeply pierced by daggers. The pain was so horrific and continuous that it was easy to convince myself that I didn't really have MS. I rationalized that if I did indeed have MS, then my body would absorb the medication and I would not be in this pain. So, therefore, I rationalized, this could not be MS.

After six weeks of injections, I couldn't stand the pain anymore. I stopped taking them and went on with my life as if I were MS-free. My family practice doctor agreed with my decision. He told me, "As humans we are responsible for taking care of ourselves, which also means knowing when to back off from something that is doing more harm than good. Benefits should outweigh the consequences, not the other way around. We are not intended to torture ourselves."

Then, a few weeks after I stopped the injections, a new symptom developed. I felt intense pain in my skin, as if someone were forcing my arms through a meat grinder until they were completely raw, and then soaking them in an acid bath. This situation was compounded by searing pains in both of my legs, from my knees down. I was in agony both with and without the medicine.

I knew something was undoubtedly wrong with me, and no medication seemed to alleviate my suffering. This wasn't fair! I wanted to know what was causing this new onslaught of pain, and I asked anyone who would listen. Unfortunately, this left me open to judgment from others who misconstrued my meaning.

My heart felt hard and bitter, a condition I knew was caused by the intense pain, fatigue and frustration. Still, I knew I could not go through life feeling this way. What could I do to make the symptoms, and my depression, better? I turned my attention back to my faith, academic classwork, and doing whatever I could to heal.

The first major change I made affected not only me, but also my entire family. It started when I altered our diet. I was determined that we all eat healthier and more nutritious foods. I continually reminded myself of the promise given to me during my near-death experience. Yes, I resolved, I would live a long life. With the help of this strong and resourceful mindset, I was able to move forward in spite of persistent neurologic symptoms.

During the fall of 2004, winter arrived with a vengeance—and with extremely low temperatures. The intense pain in my skin returned. I was uncomfortable wearing clothes. In fact, I was uncomfortable having anything touch my skin, including the blankets on my bed. Physically, it became difficult for me to walk from my car to the buildings at college. After walking a distance of about fifty feet in the cold, I was unable to grasp an exterior doorknob at the school to get into the building. Chip and I discussed the issues I was having and agreed that my symptoms seemed more incapacitating in the cold than the warm weather of the south. We decided it was time to return to Florida.

My graduation date was scheduled for the spring of 2005. I wanted to stay in Kentucky long enough to walk at my undergraduate commencement exercises. In the face of all life's potholes, I felt my attendance was a paramount milestone. How awesome would it be for my kids to know about my trials and then watch me successfully complete my degree, I reassured myself.

During my final spring term, I started round two of my research. I was amazed to gain far more results during this round than those from the prior year. In fact, at the project's conclusion, I had thousands of living lamprey larvae. When my research ended, I returned the lamprey to the location where I had collected the adults. Then I made plans to start working towards the publication of my research.

In the weeks following graduation, we packed ourselves and moved back to Florida, where Chip went back to work for his former employer at the Kennedy Space Center. Despite all of my trials, I was—and remain—so grateful for my time in Kentucky. Through those challenges, I experienced some of my greatest leaps in my personal and professional development.

When we first arrived back in Florida during the summer of 2005, we decided to rent a home so we could take the necessary time searching for our ideal "forever home". We were not having much luck until one day when I decided to drive away from the familiar roads randomly. I lost my way. As I continued driving, I saw, right in front of me, a new neighborhood still under construction. It appeared to be quiet, yet close to amenities. That afternoon, I took Chip to see it. With his approval, we signed a contract to have our house built. Yes, we did this at the peak of the economic bubble.

During March of 2006, while we were in the rental property, Chip received orders back to active duty with the military. His expected ship-out date was not until the fall, so he was home to help us move into our new home in May.

By August of 2006, I noticed potential neurological symptoms developing once again. However, I was so excited about being in my new house and getting it organized that I decided to ignore the warning signs and hoped they would go away.

In the months before we moved into our new home, I looked for a new church to attend. I located one before we moved into our house, but months passed before we actually attended our first service. In fact, we attended the church only twice before my neurological symptoms became too obvious to hide.

Regardless, I tried to ignore the symptoms because Chip was on active duty orders. I knew he couldn't help me, and I didn't want to worry him. Besides, I believed the symptoms would go away if I stopped obsessing over them. Probably, I told myself, it was just anxiety over

Chip's deployment. I knew that was something I could handle. I was wrong. Our family's darkest days were upon us.

Phoebe Walker

# Chapter 6
# Life's pivotal point

My neurological symptoms continued to spiral out of control until *THE* day that changed everything. It occurred during the fall school term of 2006, when I was thirty-three years old. After both kids left for school, my type "A" personality and I were in the bathroom getting ready for another full day. However, today turned out to be very different. When I stepped out of the shower, I dropped to the floor like the proverbial ton of bricks. This was going to be a very different kind of day, I realized immediately.

When I tried to push myself up, I realized I wasn't moving. Then I looked around to see what was preventing my movement—as if something could physically restrain me without my noticing. I realized I was stuck on the floor, which confused me since nothing visible was restraining me.

I stopped struggling for a moment and felt my heart sink as I attempted to process what was happening. "God," I asked, "what is this? What is happening to me? How long will it last? How am I supposed to respond? How can I get up?" After forcing myself back into the moment, I knew I needed help. Immediately. There was no time for fear, anger, pity, or tears. I just needed to act.

Whom should I call? We had just moved into the new construction neighborhood, and we had no neighbors on our road. Chip! I needed to call him.

It took me about thirty minutes to move the twelve feet from one side of the bathroom to the other, where I'd left my phone. My movement was peculiar, a combination of scooting, crawling, and rolling. I could not control my appendages. Finally, around nine o'clock, I managed to contact Chip at last. I apologized profusely for what was happening, but told him I really needed him. Could he help? "Please, Lord," I prayed, "let him be able to help."

Chip told me later that he could hear the fear in my voice. He immediately sought emergency leave. After the call, it took me an additional hour and a half to get myself dressed because neither my arms nor my legs were working properly. A two-year-old could dress himself or herself with better ease than I could.

The dog's bark alerted me to Chip's arrival at home, somewhere around eleven-thirty. I told myself that I needed to be closer to the door before he came in. I believed that if I were in the right place, the severity of my situation would not be so apparent. Now I'm not sure where my logic was at the time, but I honestly believed I could hide my symptoms enough to help reduce Chip's fear. After all, he was leaving the country in three weeks; he did not need to worry about this.

Chip opened the front door before I got into the "right place". His first glimpse of me was mortifying. My attempt to walk down the hallway was pitiful. What he saw were four pieces of human spaghetti slopping against the walls and floor. I could feel my legs wobbling under me, and my arms did little more than prevent my head from smashing into walls.

It is difficult for me to give a clear picture of what Chip saw because I couldn't observe it for myself. At best, I know what I felt like, and the expression in his eyes completed the story. Chip stopped in the doorway with a bag on each shoulder and one in each hand. I saw tears well up in his eyes and his jaw drop as his bags dropped to the floor. What? Didn't he see my HUGE smile, the one I carried on my face down the hall? I'd expended a great amount of energy to put that smile on my face and not cry it off the moment he walked in the front door. I guess no smile was big enough to cover the fact that I had no control over my body.

This was the first time in our marriage when I saw fear in my husband's eyes. His expression painted a painfully vivid picture of the situation. I didn't want him to be scared; I was already mortified enough for the two of us.

Somehow, with Chip at home, I knew God was near, even though I couldn't see him. Now was the time to get me to the church. That is exactly what Chip did. He took me to the church we had visited only twice. There, in the quiet, I found a profound sense of peace.

After deciding to write this book, I asked Chip what went through his mind that day when he stood in the doorway and saw me. This is what he said:

> *My initial thought when I saw you was no*
> *thought at all. I felt complete horror. I think my heart*

*dropped into my stomach, not so much about me personally, but about you. I wondered what was causing this. I desperately tried to think of a way to help you. I wondered how we were going to get through this. Then I wondered if I had done something to cause this. What could I have done differently?*

*"We just have to get through the moment. This moment," I told myself. "I need to figure out how I can I help her. What can we do to fix this? Can we fix this?"*

*I felt such anguish. "My wife is broken, and I can't fix her. How do I help her? God, I love her." Those thoughts raced through my brain. Then I thought about our kids, where they were, and what I could—and should—do for them.*

*"You need to go to the hospital. ASAP," I told you. I was upset that I hadn't been able to get home sooner. I asked myself how my family would manage. I remember thinking that the kids were going to need to help her a lot more. Can they? Will they? Those thoughts raced through my brain, in between the biggest question of all: Will my wife be able to walk again? Or will she need a wheelchair for the rest of her life?*

His answer didn't surprise me. I figured those and many other thoughts and worries were racing through his mind, fighting for attention, but giving him no time to think. No matter how desperately I tried to minimize his perceived severity of the situation, I could see in his eyes that he felt the shock and horror anyway. Nevertheless, I attempted again to play the problem off as anxiety over his deployment. I tried to reassure him that after I adjusted to his departure, everything would return to normal. We told ourselves that my symptoms might begin to settle down with him at home for two weeks on emergency leave.

We were wrong!

Eating became difficult for me because I could not hold the utensils. During his first night home, Chip made me dinner and brought it to me with a fork, knife, and spoon. This wasn't unusual; he had brought me dinner over the years. Yet on this night, I remember crying because he brought me a plate and utensils I couldn't hold. On the plate sat mashed potatoes and peas. They seemed to stare up at me.

"How can I possibly eat this?" I asked myself. Eventually I swallowed my pride, scooped some mashed potatoes with my hands, smashed them into the peas, and then shoveled the mess into my mouth. It didn't take long for Chip to realize what he had done. After profusely apologizing and shedding a few tears, he took my plate and prepared finger foods for me.

The second week Chip was home, my eyes became the center of attention. First, they began itching non-stop, to the point of distraction. The next day, that irritation compounded when my vision became blurred. As Chip's emergency leave was about to expire, my vision became much worse. However, even with the obstruction in my sight, I still had functional vision. Once again, I blamed stress for the cause of this obstruction. I continued to ignore it.

During the next two days, my peripheral vision completely disappeared. On the third day, my physical abilities disappeared. I could not do anything for myself. Once again, Chip took me to the Emergency Room.

The Emergency Room doctor determined that I was suffering from "something neurological," and gave me a steroid shot, hoping that the steroid would prevent my symptoms from getting worse. This offered minimal temporary relief. The doctor sent me home with a referral to a neurologist for follow-up treatment.

The next day, Monday, Chip drove me to see the neurologist. He ordered intravenous steroids for three days, beginning two days later. Since that would be the day Chip had to return to his duty station and I couldn't drive, he ordered a regimen of home-based infusion.

A nurse came to my home to administer the IV, but she had difficulties getting the needle into my arm. She stuck me seven times without success. One of her attempts caused me to bleed, leaving a puddle of blood on the floor the size of a Ritz cracker.

Even with limited vision, I remember the look of horror on Ashley's face as she walked in the front door after school and saw the nurse sticking me—and that was before she saw my blood all over the table and floor. I became frustrated that the woman kept trying when she was so ineffectual in hitting a vein. We exchanged words over her determination to stay and complete her work and my desire to avoid more pain and preserve my blood. When she still could not insert the

IV, I cut off the argument. I firmly told her, "You are done. Now get out of my house ... please!"

Yet I still needed to take the medication. How was I going to handle that? I had to find someone capable of starting an IV. My initial thought was the hospital. I contacted Vicki, the mother of one of Ashley's friends, who was a nurse there. She agreed to take me. The hospital could not use the IV medication I brought from my house for safety reasons. However, they were able to obtain a new prescription from the neurologist. The order called for me to go back to the hospital every twenty-four hours for administration of medication. Vicki took me the first night. Someone I vaguely knew from the church volunteered to take me the next night. My mother-in-law drove me to the hospital the last night.

I felt like I was walking in the shadow of death every time someone insisted that tomorrow would be a better day. It was such a horrible thing to hear as I watched every day get worse—for months without a break. I was so glad for one of Pastor Jim Govatos's sermons, when he addressed the scriptural meaning of "a better tomorrow". My heart melted in confirmation and relief that someone understood my situation. He explained that "scriptural tomorrow" oftentimes refers to the end of the trial, however long in human time that takes. Sometimes it can literally mean tomorrow, but most often, the time is substantially longer. In my case, it seemed never-ending. As one symptom improved, two new symptoms developed in its place.

Jim became my next silver lining. I found hope in the messages he taught.

My pain changed daily, in location and intensity, while my vision continued to deteriorate. The inability to use my hands and legs persisted. I could no longer do anything for myself physically. Soon I was blind in both eyes. My days and nights were full of blackness. I was an invalid who could not perform the simplest activities of daily living. I could not dress, feed, or clean myself. I couldn't get myself to the bathroom, open doors, or turn light switches on and off; I became a useless blob on the floor. Yet despite everything I was experiencing, I never asked why. I was sure there was a reason. Regardless of that optimism, I became so angry. I was constantly uncomfortable. I was completely helpless. And I was scared. I just wanted this nightmare to end.

I can only shake my head and imagine what my children were thinking and how terrified they were feeling. Eight-year-old Ashley was in elementary school; she was the first to leave in the morning and the first to return in the afternoon. When she arrived home from school, she felt responsible for helping me. This included taking me to my bathroom to clean me—of urine, feces, and, for several days, the added mess of menses. I still shed tears when I think about what that little girl had to endure at that young age in order to help her mother. No child should ever have to grow up that fast.

Whenever I felt sorry for myself and wanted to whine that my life wasn't fair, I recalled what Ashley was doing for me. The realization crushed my heart. I blamed myself for the life she was enduring when all she wanted to do was protect her momma by whatever means at an eight-year-old's disposal. Fortunately, she tells me she doesn't remember the worst of it.

When I ask her to reflect on what she saw and how she felt, this is what she said:

*At first, I was only thinking and hoping that Momma would get better, but as time wore on, she got worse and worse. I started to realize that I could lose my mom forever, and I thought of all the mother-daughter things we hadn't gotten to do yet. I tried to help in any way I could, hoping that little things would help her get better. When I felt like I was going to cry, I would leave Momma and go cry in my room or anywhere else where she wouldn't hear me. I felt like I had to be strong for her and do what she couldn't do, but there wasn't much an eight-year-old could do for her.*

*I felt useless and was always worrying, but I held that all inside. I didn't want to say it. Momma got worse and worse. I almost lost hope that she'd ever feel better. At the worst of the times, when I was in church, I went to the kneeling rail by myself and asked God to save my mother. Then small things showed me Momma was slowly starting to get better. I began to hope that she would live, that I would have a mother in the future, when I needed her the most.*

*Even with hope returning to me, I was still eight years old and so dreadfully afraid something would change again and turn for the worst. I constantly worried that I would never see her again. I worried about what would happen to me if something even worse happened to Momma.*

*Nevertheless, she began to improve and I began to worry less and less. Still, even to this day, I haven't stopped worrying that out of nowhere Momma could get sick again. When the worry gets too big, I have to remember to step back, take a deep breath, and pray to our dear sweet Lord to keep my Momma safe and in his loving hands.*

Because I had become a blind invalid with two young children in the home and no regular help, my husband's commanding officer told him he was not going to deploy. "I can't send you away in your current situation," the commander told Chip. Instead, he found two other individuals to take his orders; in this way, neither one had to take on the full set alone. [I send a special thanks to those who took Chip's place!!!] These two men were priceless silver linings. I have no words to express my gratitude for the sacrifice they made for us. Because of them, I didn't have to be alone in my darkness. Chip was allowed to remain in close proximity.

Chip was still on active duty orders, though, and his commanding officer instructed him to remain with his command until the orders expired. The base was several hours away, but Chip continued to make road trips several days a week. This made it possible for him to accompany me to my medical appointments and for him to help with the children as well as with me. Three months passed before Chip was able to transfer his military work location. At the new location, he was close enough to our house that he could comfortably commute daily. He continued this way until the end of his orders in March 2007.

It became apparent to both of us that we needed to research MS and learn as much as we could about the disease. I needed to identify what factors and activities made it worse and what lessened the severity of my symptoms. We clearly needed direction in how to move forward. The next chapter shares much of what we learned about this disease.

Phoebe Walker

# Chapter 7
# What is MS, anyway?

Chip had to carry me into the office the first day I met my new neurologist in the fall 2006. I could not walk, much of my vision was gone, and I didn't have a wheel chair. The doctor ordered an MRI of my brain, to see what changes had taken place. The MRI revealed that I had more than 75 lesions between my brain and my spine, many of them still active. These absolutely confirmed our fears. The doctor diagnosed me with Multiple Sclerosis—the third time I had heard those words from doctors.

This time I was not shocked and I did not fight the diagnosis. I just wanted to live. I was ready to accept the news and learn to live with the verdict. I was prepared to dance in a hurricane. I continue the dance today.

We all have white blood cells that help fight infection. In normal people, when the infection is defeated, the white blood cells park themselves until they have another bug to go fight. In a person with Multiple Sclerosis, however, the white blood cells do not stop their work; they continue to chew away at tissue, even though it is healthy tissue. The medical world calls these sites lesions, holes in the protective covering of a nerve. This creates a disconnection in the message that goes from the brain to each respective body part.

To address my blindness, the neurologist sent me to a neuro-ophthalmologist. That specialist confirmed that I was suffering from optic neuritis, a swelling of the optic nerve. This is one of the key symptoms in MS, and the swelling had blinded me to the point that my world was black.

When I discuss MS, I explain that a lesion is similar to the wire on a lamp or any other electronic device. When the wire is missing the rubber outer edge, sometimes the device turns on, sometimes it does not, and yet other times the device will flicker between off and on. This phenomenon continues to worsen the longer the device is turned on, because the exposed wire gets hot. That, in turn, means that electrical messages are not relayed completely, which prevents the device from functioning properly. That same response happens with the nerves in a person with MS. Sometimes we are able to function well, and sometimes we do not, while other times we are just flat-out unsure of what to expect.

I have discovered that environmental climates also affect my abilities. Using the wire analogy again, if the wire/nerve becomes too hot or cold, then symptoms are exacerbated. Some people with MS can tolerate cold better than heat, while others find the reverse is true for them. However, I believe most people find the greatest complications coming most likely from a variation of extreme temperatures.

Those complications can lead to difficulties walking, swallowing, or speaking. We may experience a prickly or burning sensation in our skin, vision disturbances or complete loss of sight, spasticity, incontinence, pain, and a plethora of other symptoms. Some are treatable, but generally only with medications that come with their own set of side effects. I tend to "walk" through the symptoms without the medications, because I think the side effects are far worse.

The drive to the neuro-ophthalmologist's office seemed never-ending, because I couldn't see where we were going or if we were almost there. This was the longest distance I had ridden in a car without any eyesight, which may have contributed to my elevated anxiety. I kept asking Chip if we were close and if not, how much time remained. He said I reminded him of a child asking, "Are we there yet? ... Are we there yet?" He told me my questions were cute. He made it his job to try to keep a smile on my face with his attempts at humor, but maybe it was to help put a smile on his face, too. When I wasn't thinking about where we were, I was worrying that the doctor was going to tell me I would be blind forever.

Looking back on that experience now, I am amazed that after being able to see clearly for thirty-three years, I never realized or fully appreciated eyesight and its role in my daily life. Without vision, I had no concept of time, which made even the infinitesimal things seem to take forever. As an artist and painter, I found that one of the most difficult side effects was the loss of color. No matter how hard I tried, I could not visualize color or shapes. Everything was just black—not levels or variations of black, but the darkest black I have ever experienced. Better yet, it was the absolute absence of light and sight. It was disconcerting, unnerving, even frightening never to know if someone was near me, who it was, where I was, or what people were doing around me.

While I waited to see the doctor, worries swirled around in my head. I kept thinking there was a real possibility that my sight would never return. I even questioned whether my blindness was caused by MS, because I had been told that optic neuritis was only supposed to affect one eye at a time. Yet I was profoundly blind in both eyes.

The moment of truth arrived as I was sitting in the exam chair and the doctor asked if I could see how many fingers he was holding up. Swallowing my fear, I somberly replied, "I can't see anything." Then I heard clinking noises. The doctor explained that he was going to look into my eyes with a very bright light. Hope! There was hope for a minute because this is what I had been waiting for.

In the past, this light had been painfully bright. Surely, I thought, I would at least be able to see a hint of light. With his hand on my forehead, I began to *will* myself to see the light. After what seemed like a long time had passed and I had not seen anything, I asked, "Is the light on yet?"

The three people in the room replied with unilateral confirmation, "YES!"

**BAM!** My world broke in two. Darkness and devastation covered me and imbedded an inexplicable level of fear. I found myself swallowing. Hard. I could hear my loud gulp as I pondered how I was going to live as a blind person.

"We need some baseline tests," the doctor told Chip and me. He sent me for a visual field test. Here they put the patient's head in a dome-shaped machine, cover one eye, and place a clicker in the patient's hand. In the dome, the patient faces straight ahead. As lights appear, the patient clicks the button. In this way, the doctor can identify the individual's field of vision.

I could not tell whether I was looking straight ahead; I think I even asked the technician if I was. After sitting through these tests previously, I knew what to expect. As the process began, I felt so frustrated that I was unable to see any of the lights that I actually contemplated pushing the clicker regardless. As I listened to the "poor-me" fit developing in my head, I heard sniffles coming from behind me. My heart dropped to the floor.

I was broken, and Chip could see it. Now he was sobbing because he knew he couldn't fix me. I didn't want to be blind. How could I be his partner through life if I couldn't see? I felt as if I had just become a huge burden to this very hard-working and loving man. I tried not to think about what this would do to my children. The situation overwhelmed me. Now I could hear that it overwhelmed him, too.

The doctor's final comment on the issue gave me a smidgen of relief: he confirmed that he believed my blindness was due to MS. "We'll just have to play the waiting game and hope for the best," he said, patting me on the arm. "If the vision loss is caused by the MS, that means it is most likely temporary."

The question became how long would I have to wait? I have to admit, I find it difficult to identify the silver lining for this storm. Certainly, Chip made sure I was taken care of and safe, but my only survival tools at this time were to cling to belief and faith while continuing to live as best I could.

# Chapter 8
# The servants

In October of 2006, I was completely blind, my husband was away from home four or five nights each week, I had two young children at home, and we didn't know many people in the area. Our house was in a new neighborhood in Titusville, Florida, with no other homes completed on my road. How was I going to take care of my kids if I couldn't even take care of myself? I worried that the state was going to take my children from me.

At that time, TJ was in middle school. He was last to leave in the morning and last to return home after school. On school days after he left, I sat on a couch in the front room, with one dog on either side of me like little cherubs. I remained there until either I slid myself to the floor or my daughter returned in the afternoon.

Six long hours stretched between the time when TJ left in the morning and Ashley came home in the afternoon. Many times, I just sat and cried, especially after I was incontinent. This humiliation deepened my depression. I mocked myself for being a baby and commented that maybe someone should buy me diapers; it would make everyone's job easier. No matter how deep I dug within my soul, I found no nice words to say to myself. Additionally, I refused to talk to others because I didn't feel worthy. I felt dirty.

As the time neared for Ashley to arrive home, I felt a huge sense of dread about what she would see when she walked through the door. The circumstances were completely unfair for my young daughter to endure. I decided to refrain from eating or drinking because I wanted to reduce my waste. I did not want this life for her, but I was helpless to make any changes. Fortunately, her heart was strong enough to handle it. She has always been a silver lining in my life—and I was—and continue to be—acutely aware of her sacrifices during this time.

Of everyone in my family, I was most concerned about my son. He was openly angry about my situation, and I couldn't help him or do anything to change things. This was evident on several occasions. For instance, when I went into the kitchen, he would trap me in my wheelchair between objects. Around the island, he often placed a bag of garbage behind me and the trash can in front of me, and then he left the room. I remained trapped until someone came to move the barricades; most of the time, that was Ashley.

At the time, TJ was too angry to articulate how he felt. He was in middle school and seemed to hate being there. He always came home angry, never did his schoolwork, and refused to talk about the causes of his anger. Several years later, he told me it was because he always had bad days at school and then came home to a sick mother. He said he had not paid enough attention in science class to the lessons on cancer, and he thought MS was like having cancer. If I had known he was comparing the two, I might have been able to help him understand they were not the same.

TJ tells me that his most vivid memories of those days focused on the way my condition continued to worsen, to the point where we needed help from others because we didn't have family nearby. "I was afraid you might die," he told me later. His feelings of helplessness, fear, concern, and embarrassment overwhelmed and confused him. Fortunately, a time came, months later, when he realized things were starting to get better.

Of course, I would have done anything to prevent this hurt that caused so much confusion and pain for my son. He may have lashed out at me in anger during this time, but I understand it was only because he was hurt and didn't know how to articulate his feelings. Fortunately, he no longer has those conflicting feelings about me.

One day in the fall of 2006, I received a phone call from a woman at the church we had just started to attend. She explained that she knew we were in the middle of a difficult life situation and asked if she could help. I wondered how she knew about our troubles. I hadn't told anyone. At first, pride got in the way and I started thinking, "How can I let anyone help me? What will they think of me after I let them close enough to see everything about me?" Then my thoughts shifted to the kids. I knew we desperately needed the help, so I told her I would be grateful to receive their assistance.

The caller was a member of a discipleship group. Our church had several running simultaneously. This woman made contact with every discipleship group and arranged dinners for four nights a week, which continued for about three months. An attorney at the church offered to help us with legal disability benefits (which had been denied to me). Other people offered to help with my kids, especially when they needed rides from school. Once, a women's group came to clean my house.

Of the many wonderful people who helped me during those months of great need, one of the most amazing was Leanne. She just sat with me. I wondered how she could feel comfortable just sitting there in the dark, my darkness, and expect little to no conversation for hours. I love this woman for the sacrifice she offered; she made me feel priceless. That was the kind of love many of us don't know how to express, but unconditional love is the greatest blessing we can receive. Once I swallowed my pride, I welcomed anyone willing to join me in my darkness.

Surprisingly, once I let people help us, the most difficult part for me was the picture they revealed to me of our situation. While they never actually told me, I could hear their shock, fear, and concern in their voices and sniffling noses. I knew they were sobbing because of my situation. Looking back, I feel fortunate to have had that many people who cared deeply enough to share so much of my pain.

During the healing process, countless total strangers stepped up to help us, overwhelming me with a depth of love I had never received before. This love manifested itself into a truly beautiful picture that brought me immense peace.

Though relief came with these wonderful people, I was still too uncomfortable to sleep much. During those interminable sleepless hours, I prayed for everyone who was praying for me and I prayed for anyone else who came into my mind, even people from my past as far back as I could remember. For a while, I went down memory lane, connecting with memories of friends as far back as pre-school, elementary school, and middle school. To me, all these people represented individual silver linings, rays of hope that projected me forward. Eventually, I didn't need to pray for my healing, because so many others had me covered. That is when I noticed a dramatic change for the positive.

Phoebe Walker

# Chapter 9
# Encounter with an Angel

After nearly four months, the healing began. Although I was still not well enough to take care of myself, I desperately wanted to be present for my kids in a positive way throughout their daily lives. During the Christmas season, TJ had a band concert at school, and that became a special moment during a bleak time. Chip was home, so he packed my wheelchair, the kids, and me into the truck and we went to the school together. It was like a breath of fresh air to get out of the house for something other than doctors' appointments and church.

My positive outlook changed, however, soon after we arrived at the school. I felt like I was an embarrassment to TJ, and I felt smothered as people crowded around me. Because of my months of seclusion and minimal vision, the room sounded like Grand Central Station in the middle of rush hour. After I had grown accustomed to quiet and darkness, the sensation made me alarmingly dizzy. The conversations taking place around me filled my head with a million thoughts that I could not stop. Where were these thoughts before I opted to go out of the house?

When I was a child, I was very shy. Then I moved in with my dad and actively transformed myself into a social butterfly. My need to get out and be social must have been too much to handle that night. Yet

I desperately wanted to be present as a mother for my child. Those two desires were so strong that they caused me to overrule any concerns that this might be too much stimulation too soon.

Each student had one parent sit next to him or her as the student played in the concert. I wanted to be that parent for TJ, but I could not because of the wheelchair. What compounded the issue was that I could not focus my eyes on any one thing. Because so much was going on around me, I opted to stare at the floor. I felt isolated and vulnerable because Chip was sitting with TJ and Ashley went off to find her friends. I sat alone while people walked around me as if I were a fixture on the floor.

Regardless of the overwhelming sensations on this outing, it was a good first step in building a forward momentum. After this night, each consecutive outing built on the last, helping me identify ways to make day-to-day living a little easier. After that outing, I started to identify what went wrong during a trip and what I could do next time to avoid the obstacle. Confidence built in me through each of these learning processes.

As my vision started to return, I thought I saw something move in my extreme peripheral vision. I decided to experiment by reaching my right arm over my head and wiggling my fingers. YES! I could see them! Oh my goodness, imagine the excitement when I realized there was a correlation between my hand gestures and my vision of movement! I couldn't tell what I was seeing, but when I wiggled my fingers, I could see shadows move. Better yet, both eyes registered the same response.

Rejoicing that I was no longer confined to solid blackness, I constantly did the "wiggle my fingers over my head" to remind myself that at least I had some semblance of vision. Upon experimenting in different lighting, I learned that I couldn't see as well in bright light as in darker surroundings. I am sure my actions annoyed a few people. In fact, I remember people asking what I was doing. One person actually said it was annoying and asked if I would please cease and desist.

Although some vision was returning, I remained legally blind. Regardless, I felt that life was good. Every day for weeks, I noticed sporadic spots appear in my vision. Each one was like a single piece of a puzzle. I waited excitedly for a bazillion more to complete the picture. Though my vision improved, it remained compromised by my inability to see lights or color. Large holes remained in my vision, and I had no perception of depth. These limitations were frustrating, and I began getting impatient. I started wondering whether this was it, the new me, or if I could bargain to have more vision restored.

My hope began to waver. The only way to obtain new hope in such a dismal time was to connect with my faith, I knew. One day I sat on the floor and started singing "Amazing Grace." Then I planted my face on the floor as I prayed to God and searched for one conceptual living blade of thriving grass to pierce through my floor. I knew I would not find a literal blade of grass growing through my carpet, but I was desperately seeking hope.

In my search, something swept over me. What was it? I heard my quivering voice say, "God, as long as my blindness and inabilities are going to help someone else somehow, then I am willing to stay this way as long as necessary."

"Wow! Did I really just say that?" I asked myself.

I felt the need to sing again, and I sang "Amazing Grace" with as much intensity and emotion as I could muster. Time seemed to stand still. Suddenly I felt compelled to look up to the sky. When I did, I received a divine peace that immersed my entire core deeply. In that moment, I felt endowed with answers to questions I didn't know I had. I'm sure this sounds confusing – it was for me, too. Yet, despite my confusion, I understood that everything was going to be all right, that my condition was not going to be permanent. I sent up praises of thanksgiving that it was God's plan to restore me.

Then, out of nowhere, about four feet from where I sat on the floor, I saw the most beautiful blue silhouette of an adult-sized human shape, void of features, sitting in a chair. How could I see it? I hadn't been able to see light or color, yet I saw this color, and it was glowing. I felt compelled to speak. "I don't know who or what you are," I said, "but I can feel a supernatural presence with you here."

I never heard an audible word spoken. I felt the need to close my eyes and hold on tight, because my God was in control of this ride. Once again, I sang "Amazing Grace" with as much of my soul as I could put into the song. As I sang, I felt an inexplicable peace fill me. The knot in my stomach dissolved. I had no sense of time. I didn't want the angel to go away, because it brought a peace and comfort that could only have come from Heaven. To this day, I feel choked up when I think of this experience.

I didn't tell people about the angel, for fear of what they would think. Even though I was certain of the peace that washed over me, I was still uncertain of what I had seen, which made me uncomfortable about discussing the experience with any authority. A few weeks later, my minister, Pastor Jim Govatos, delivered a sermon on angels. He said that angels do exist. I realized it was possible that I really did see what I thought I saw.

The visit from this angel completely changed my life. From that experience forward, my physical condition improved more rapidly. Unlike the first time I asked God into my heart, this experience changed my heart overnight. I felt an increase in my tolerance level for all people who acted or thought differently. I came to believe that every person is truly worthy of being forgiven and loved, no matter how difficult they are to achieve.

I was completely humbled. Additionally, I realized that our hardships are necessary, preparing us to help others through similar situations. My physical brokenness would allow me to become someone else's silver lining. From this epiphany, I started referring to my MS as a blessing, not a curse. However, I still desperately wanted the disease to go away; no part of MS is desirable.

Phoebe Walker

# Chapter 10
# Healing Takes Place

About a month into my invalid state, I realized that I needed to make a physical attempt to help heal my body. We had a treadmill in the living room. When Chip was home, I asked him to position me on the treadmill, with the top half of my body draped over the controls and the emergency shut-off cord attached to a belt loop on my pants. He turned the treadmill on to its lowest setting. In this way, as my feet were dragged behind me by the treadmill belt, I attempted to drag my feet forward, one at a time. That was excruciatingly difficult work to perform. However, after only a couple of weeks, I was able to stand up by myself on the treadmill and put one foot in front of the other in time with the belt. I didn't care how shaky those steps were, at least I was progressing in the right direction.

In September 2006, my next silver lining appeared. Kachina Childs came to live with us. We had met while I was a student at Campbellsville University in Campbellsville, Kentucky, between 2002 and 2005. When she came to our house, she brought her baby girl. Because two additional people also brought a financial obligation we couldn't meet alone, she got a job to carry that weight. Her new job significantly limited the time she had available to help us, but we were so appreciative of any time she was available.

We still joke about how much help she truly was, but honestly, the humor she brought us delivered healing for everyone. One night, on a weekend when Chip was home, we went out for dinner at Sonny's Restaurant. I could walk, but I was still legally blind. Kachina wanted to help me by being my guide person; she called herself my seeing-eye dog. As she escorted me to my seat, she walked me into almost everything—people, chairs, and the buffet.

I thought I was safe when we left the restaurant and were heading to the truck. The walk was smooth, and we successfully cleared the exit doors without incident. I was confident we were going to get to the truck without a situation. Then, BAM. I had run into something solid, and I could hear ringing in my ears. I shouted in laughter, "What in the world? Where did that come from?" Yep, Kachina had walked me into the pole of a disabled sign in the parking lot.

Was this woman doing it on purpose? No. Kachina is not that kind of person – though she has more than her fair share of moments like this. She brought some much-needed comedy relief. Everyone laughed so hard, it was cleansing to the soul.

My best spiritual connections take place at the church altar and at the ocean. I attribute my greatest healing moments to the peace I absorb while in God's presence on the beach. I go there to feel his physical touch, to feel his full embrace. When I was at my worst, I had someone guide me to both places.

One of my most amazing spiritual connections took place one evening at the beach with Kachina. When we arrived, she helped me hobble to the spot where the waves met the dry sand. Despite my limited vision, moonlight made it possible for me to see the white tips of the waves. They looked like God's fingertips—and that thought caused my heart to skip a beat as my eyes connected with them.

This was the first time I had been to the ocean since I had become blind and disabled, which made it a truly special moment. I remember positioning myself where I could feel soggy wet sand—the kind that feels like quicksand—under my feet. This let me know that I was in the "Spiritual Touch Zone." I awaited the waves.

Just as the water crashed into my shins, I cried out for comfort and fell to my knees in the surf. As the current pulled out and the new waves crashed back on me, I knew that God was present, wrapping his arms around me like a loving parent. He was binding the fear and pain and dragging them far away.

When it was time to go home, we realized I was soaked to the bone and we had neither a towel nor dry clothes. Fortunately, the pier where we parked was right next to Ron Jon's Surf Shop, which operates twenty-four hours a day. We decided to make a pit stop there, to purchase dry clothes and a towel, so I could be more comfortable on the forty-five-minute trip back home.

The night was memorable for another reason. Thanks to the outing, I slept better than I had in months. I cannot describe what a gift substantive sleep is after months where I could not doze off for more than minutes or an hour at a time.

———

Kachina and I made another trip to the beach one night after she came home from work and realized I'd had a rough day. By that time, my sight was functional for getting around on my own without running into things though walking resembled a hobbling troll. The day had not been an easy one. Kachina decided she would treat me to a beach outing.

This gesture started as a good deed and ended with a legal repercussion. You see, when we reached the beach, she wanted to park as close to the walkway as she could so I wouldn't have to walk too far. The problem was that she parked illegally in a no-parking zone. Darkness had already fallen outside and no one was around, we reasoned, so what were the odds that a police officer would drive past? Call it our unlucky night. After our time on the beach, we returned to the truck to discover a ticket under the wiper blade. I was just glad the truck wasn't towed.

However, the problem did not stop there. I was still having physical issues with my hands, which prevented me from writing a check—or writing anything, for that matter. This forced me to delay paying the ticket for a couple of weeks. After delaying as long as I could, I realized no matter how hard I tried, I could not *will* myself to do something that physically was impossible. I made multiple attempts to write something – anything. No matter how hard I tried, my fingers flat-out refused to make anything that resembled a number or letter.

I finally conceded to my inability and asked Kachina to write the check for me. Then I scribbled nonsense for a signature and said,

"Perfect. Now the bank will know for sure it came from me. Ha! Let's see how far it flies." After I mailed the check to the city, I decided I should probably contact the bank and explain that they would be getting a check with scribbles. "Please accept it," I asked. And they did.

When my vision returned enough for me to see objects and my physical abilities improved enough to allow me some independence, I began attempting to tackle chores. I walked around my house intentionally looking for something that I could do. When I found a small piece of lint or trash on the floor, I picked it up and threw it away. At last, I had found some way to help my family. While that activity level did not match my former pre-disability level of family caretaker, it was a step in the right direction—literally. No matter how mundane my accomplishments were, I celebrated each of my increasing abilities.

The first day I was able feed myself, I ate at the dinner table, using utensils for the first time. When I finished eating, I got up, carefully pushed my chair in, grabbed my plate and silverware, and walked toward the sink. Every step was slow and carefully thought out, because my hands were occupied. I knew that if I fell, I would not be able to catch myself before hitting the floor.

Chip turned around and was startled by what he saw. He reached out to take my dishes, but I smiled at him and said, "No! I want to do it by myself. Please let me." Then I added, "Look! I'm *DOING* it! *ALL … BY … MYSELF!*" I cried many tears from the pride I felt for this tremendous accomplishment. It was as if I had learned to walk for the first time.

My steps may have been slow and heavy, but I got where I intended to go. This began my first real contribution to cleaning up after myself since my MS episode started. I cannot remember the exact timing, but this was probably five months after my initial nerve-related symptoms.

Once my vision started returning at an accelerated rate, I decided to draw a picture, knowing people would be amazed by what I saw. However, I never accomplished that goal. Initially, only one segment of my vision completely returned as a solid picture, and that was the extreme peripheral. My eyesight was much like trying to see a full picture though a pinhole—but from the side, not the middle.

The center of my vision returned only one speck at a time. At first, it was easy to notice new specks because I was starting with a solid black background. Sporadic specks slowly appeared in no particular order or location, like a black-and-white picture covered with hundreds of holes. Everything remained black and white. I had no depth perception, and lots of missing pieces. Regardless of the choppy view, though, I celebrated every new piece of restored vision.

Before I lost my sight, I enjoyed carving surfboard shapes out of 36"x 12" rectangular pieces of wood. My intention was to shape, sand, and paint them. I was in the middle of sanding three boards when the disability began. Though I could not paint the pictures on them without my eyesight, I realized I could sand them. There was no better time than now to start sanding, I decided, because I didn't need my eyes for this activity. In fact, I think my inability to see the boards made for a much smoother surface. I relied on my sense of touch, rather than eyesight, and they became the smoothest boards I have produced to date.

One of the boards is currently hanging on my wall, I sold one on E-Bay, and the other is at MADD Jack's Grillin Shack restaurant in Cocoa Beach, Florida; the shack is voted the fourth best barbeque restaurant in the U.S. by Trip Advisor.[2] Not only was this craft something I could do, the boards serve as reminders of where I was. They offered a vision of hope, healing, and personal growth. During that somber time in my life, it was good to feel like I had some purpose, something to create when so much had been taken away. What is even better is that I still have access to two of the boards whenever I want.

About six months after my first visit with the neuro-ophthalmologist, I had my first follow-up appointment. This one found me back in front of that dome for another visual field test. Chip and I

---

[2] Madd Jacks contact information is in appendix A.

were flipping through magazines to pass time while we waited to for our call into the exam room. What a difference six months had made! I cannot describe how wonderful I felt this time, in comparison. I could actually see again. Well … for the most part, I could.

One of the magazine advertisements showed a picture of grilled meat. I got excited and shouted, "Grilled chickie!"

Chip chuckled and said, "Nope, that's sausage."

We came to another meat advertisement, I said, "Okay, I didn't get the last one, but I've got this one – this one IS chickie – cluck cluck!"

My husband began laughing so hard he nearly fell out of his chair. "Nope," he said. "That's the same picture as the last one."

When I flipped to the back page, I found yet another picture of grilled meat. I briefly considered whether or not I should guess this one, because I had missed the last two. However, I was so confident in my answer that I shouted, "This one is pig – oink oink."

He said, "Nope, that's cow … moo." Maybe my vision wasn't as good as I thought it was, but it sure provided a humorous moment. Now, the running joke is that I cannot keep my poultry, cows, and pigs straight. Apparently, to me, at one time they all looked the same.

Eventually I decided I had enough vision to attempt painting. I spent three weeks painting a design that under normal circumstances would have taken me only three hours to complete. The delay was caused by my lack of depth perception. I couldn't tell when the end of the paintbrush was touching the board—and that was a serious challenge. I went through all the stages of frustration and anger when the paint did not come off the brush onto the board—and then I realized the brush wasn't even touching the surface. Other times, out of impatience, I over-compensated by pressing the brush extra hard, leaving globs of paint on the board. Another challenge was my visual color palette: I could only see the gray scale, which meant I needed assistance with paint colors.[3] Ashley was my helper for this. When I asked for a color, she put it on a paper plate and brought it to me.

I was extremely excited and felt blessed to regain so many abilities, but I also had many frustrations. I wanted more. In time, I realized that no matter how good I was at doing something or accomplishing something on my own, I should always be open and accepting of help from others.

Throughout the healing time, I regularly checked to see if my vision was good enough to move to the next step. More than six months had passed since I last drove. One day I thought my vision was restored enough to attempt this milestone. I wanted to start slowly, so I chose a short distance with straight roads and minimal traffic. Before climbing into the vehicle, though, I failed to take into consideration the overcast sky, which severely decreased my already limited vision—remember also that I still couldn't see lights when I looked directly at them.

---

[3] My website has photos of my paintings. Web address is in appendix A.

All was going well until I drove down a road that required me to keep to the left in order to avoid the building traffic in the right lane. I slammed on the brakes, and I think my heart stopped beating. There had been an accident. About forty feet in front of me sat a police car with all its lights flashing. Yes, lights that I could not see because they became invisible when I looked directly at them.

I crept the vehicle forward to the spot where the police officer fervently gestured for me to stop – with his finger. I rolled my window down. "Didn't you see me here?" he demanded to know.

I realized that I needed to respond carefully. Out came "I do now. Yes, sir."

"You should have your eyes examined," he suggested, and sent me on my way.

As I drove off, I guessed it was a good thing I hadn't told him that I'd had my eyes examined the week before. He might have taken my license away on the spot. When I returned home, I conceded that it was entirely too soon for me to drive. I hung up my keys, grateful nothing worse had happened.

By the summer of 2007, about nine months after my initial onset of disabilities, nearly eighty percent of my vision had returned and I had regained my abilities to do most things for myself. God was the source behind this healing—my abilities all started returning on their own several months before the doctors prescribed regular three-times-a-week medications.

Despite that significant level of healing, sometimes I could not control the force behind my body's actions. One day when someone rang the doorbell, I tried to run from the back of the house to the front door before the person left. What actually happened went something like this: thud, step, smack, thud, step, smack. The leg I could not control landed where it wanted to, followed by the power of the good leg propelling me forward and consequently slamming me into the wall. I did this for a distance of about thirty feet.

Once I reached the front door and opened it, I could not stop myself. Out the front door I flew, looking for anything to halt my forward momentum. Ah, ha! There was a palm tree in the middle of the front yard. I reached my arm out like a hook. Yep, worked like a charm. It catapulted me straight at the front of the house. Forward I went, right through the flowerbed, where I took out the garden gnome and smacked into the wall at the doorbell. Okie dokie, I was now stopped—to the utter astonishment of my visitor. I decided to make a mental note that next time I should attempt to approach the front door a bit more slowly.

Once I was no longer running around like a wild banshee, I could hear hearty laughter. The person who rang my doorbell was half standing, half falling against the wall, laughing and snorting so hard he was crying. No matter, he was entirely too amused by what he had just seen. He could do little more than hold his gut.

A few weeks later, my comedy reel ran again. This time it began with the phone ringing. I ran toward the room to the left of the front door, taking the same path I had used previously, when I accidentally flew out the front door. This time my legs were doing much better, so the run was not an issue. However, I overshot where I was supposed to turn. Fortunately, I corrected my path just before I ran into the wall. This was only a minor detour. I simply went past the coffee table and turned to come back toward the corner next to the couch. As I reached to grab the phone, I lost my balance and flipped backwards over the arm of the couch. I landed folded in half, with my back on the wall and my butt on the floor. To add insult to injury, I was unsuccessful at answering the phone before the caller hung up.

Surely, I thought, in my failure to answer the phone in time, I should have at least earned some sort of reward for that perfect half-pike that took place over the edge of the couch. It was flawless! Kidding, of course, but those were the moments I wish I could have recorded to replay whenever I wanted some real-time humor in the middle of my valley. Yes, having MS can bring very ugly days. But I have to tell you, I have found so much joy, love, and humor in my attempt to combat this disease. I *choose* to have more good days than bad, so I will continue to seek out the good and focus on the funny moments rather than the tragic ones.

Whenever I started having an exacerbation of neurological symptoms, my doctor ordered a high dose of intravenous steroids, coordinated to work with my regular three-times-a-week injections. The IV medication reduces swelling of my nerves, which helps reduce the symptoms. When he ordered the intravenous medication, I went to an infusion center to have it administered.

Comedy relief followed me to the infusion center, not only from my body's own malfunctioning, but also from that of the individuals who occupied my space. For instance, I think Chip was always trying to pay me back for something I didn't do. You see, there was something in the infusion center that triggered his fart gland. No kidding, every time we went, there was some sort of fart-a-thon coming from his tail end. To this day, I do not know what triggers it. Perhaps this is something divinely intended to lighten the mood – a divine wind.

On one of our visits to the infusion center, Chip started sniffing the air around him. I asked what he was doing. "Someone just farted near me," he said. That was, funny, because we were in a private room and no one was near us. Besides, I could not smell anything. Then he stood up and walked to the door to see if he could identify the source of the odor. Oh, my goodness, I think I was smacked in the face with a fart-nugget and the IV prevented me from moving fast enough to get away, so I just stayed down and covered my face with the blanket. "Chip – it burns!" I chuckled. My eyes were burning and my gut-wrenching laughter caused me to dribble on myself. I was a hot mess.

One of my nurses, Sylvia, was in the room next door during the commotion. When she peeked around the corner, I told her that Chip was blaming someone else for his own flatulence. Unable to hold her own composure, she laughed and warned him, "You better not bring that out into the hallway. Just keep it in there."

Chip could not help himself. He wanted to share. From the door, he started jumping into the hallway and back into my room several times, just to stir the eau de fart scent into the hallway. I am not sure, but I think they had to call in a HAZMAT team to sanitize that space before they could bring in a new patient. I'm joking, of course, but really, days like this brought forth some of the best healing. Humor has definitely been one of my silver linings.

To see my actual healing was wonderful and uplifting. Having fun on the journey made the hard times tolerable. Now that restoration was about complete, it was time to start thinking about the next step for me. What would my new life look like?

# Chapter 11
# A New Start

Before the entire MS thing railroaded me like a freight train in the fall of 2006, Chip was about to deploy overseas with the military, and we were actively preparing for his departure. This process included getting financial affairs in order, making sure we had all the accurate emergency contact information, up-to-date power of attorney, living wills, and contact information for military ombudsmen.

As the spouse of a member of the military, whenever I knew he was going away, I intentionally planned things that would occupy my mind. It always helped our time apart to go much faster. This time I wanted the activity to be something fun that would occupy me for the entire duration of his six-month deployment and culminate in something special for all of us on the other end. We were about to celebrate our ten-year anniversary, so I thought, "Let's do a vow renewal."

We almost canceled our plans because of my physical struggles, but, fortunately, we persevered with them. The months-long preparations for this ceremony were stored in boxes that were lost in a corner somewhere after the disease came and crushed me. Many months later, in the spring of 2007, I felt strong enough to ask myself, "Should I pull the boxes out and resume the preparations?"

Was I crazy to go ahead with this? I believed not.

The truth is my life was drastically shaken to levels I did not know were tolerable. Then, like Bette Midler's song *Wind Beneath My Wings*, I would turn behind me and realize that Chip was standing there. He could have left at any point. Chip worked full time at a civilian job and full time at his military job, in addition to running around full time with my medical needs and the kids' schedules. To compound his schedule further, he continued to keep up with his own fitness by working out almost daily. I imagine that helped him cope with all his responsibilities.

Chip could have used his hectic life as an excuse to refuse to help me with any of the medical procedures I went through. He could have denied me the opportunities to move around looking for the right climate for the disease. Yes, he could have given up at any point along the way. But he did not. That man has a level of love for me that is difficult to find. I know I received the absolute best when Chip was designated as my earthly partner. I wanted the world to know that, so I wrote my vows for the vow renewal service.[4]

Yes, we needed to celebrate, and we needed to do it big. Okay, there were times I thought I was crazy because, though the timing was

---

[4] The entire vow renewal ceremony is printed in Appendix C.

spot on, the workload was difficult. I did most of the preparations alone and easily tired during the process.

I asked Rana to be my matron of honor for this vow renewal. She and I had maintained a strong sisterly relationship over the years since we met in 1994, during my first marriage. Chip and I had been married by a Justice of the Peace in March 1997; in December of that year, Rana and Cristi had been in our wedding. This time around, we decided to have a very different wedding ceremony, and we asked Rana to participate. In retrospect, I should have also contacted Cristi to be in this renewal-of-vows service. The reason may be as simple as I only included people who had helped me during my incapacitated times. Regardless, Rana became my matron of honor and planned an extended three-week stay at my house. She flew in from Ohio and helped me with the final details. I could not have pulled everything together without her.

I'm not sure where my special fascination with Hawaii came from. I've never been there, although I feel a special peace when I think about it. Maybe I love it because the ocean fully encompasses the islands that make up Hawaii, and the ocean is one of the places where I find deep spiritual peace. Regardless of its origins, I used my passion for Hawaii as the central theme of the vow-renewal celebration. I researched the Hawaiian faith and faith rituals, along with their meanings and uses. I also researched the islands and wove many intricate details into a beautiful celebration.

Every detail I chose to incorporate held great significance to me. In fact, each one became a drop in my bucket for leaving the past behind and the bucket of hope for a better, more solid future—the kind of future one attains with solid roots in the ground. Visualize the effort that I put into each of the intricate details. The amount of energy I spent on each one directly corresponded with the energy I was investing into starting my life again. It was hard work, but fun—and with many rewards.

This vow renewal was different from our first wedding in 1997, when there were entirely too many conflicts among family members. Those conflicts led to several uncomfortable moments during our reception. This time, we wanted only those people who were optimistic and conflict-free to celebrate with us. We made two exceptions to our policy of no family in attendance. The first was my dad, because he had contacted me about three months into my blindness. Once he learned of my situation, he maintained regular contact with me and did what he could to help from Indiana. Second were the parents of my stepmom, Sherry. John and Nancy have a marriage that Chip and I aspire to emulate.

Our bottom line for attendance was this: we only wanted people who had been actively involved in our healing process. They surrounded and loved us throughout those difficult days in a way I had not previously known was humanly possible. Our choice of guests was perfect, because not only were we celebrating our anniversary, but we were also celebrating the recovery of my lost physical abilities.

The vow renewal was beautiful, thanks in part to the Hawaiian traditions we incorporated into the service. I ordered fresh flowers shipped in from Hawaii. We held the ceremony on the beach, under an arched huppa with sheer white fabric draped over the top and embellished with greenery and flowers. On either side of the huppa, three tiki torches were filled with flowers. Under the huppa sat a table with a large open shell that held two fresh flower leis and one lei made of green tea leaves, which we used in our lasso ceremony.

Also on the table under the huppa were two small shells, each filled with different colored sands. Chip had blue sand, I had white sand, and the central jar had earth-color sand, to represent God. We alternated pouring our sand into the jar to represent our complete spiritual connection. This ceremony replaced candle lighting because we could not light candles on the beach.

Okay, so every planned event generally has a few minor glitches. Ours had quite a few, but I think they made the event a perfect representation of what we were celebrating. It was the culmination of a season with major life struggles, from which we were emerging into a beautiful new beginning on the other side. This was a celebration of brokenness transformed into wholeness, in both our marriage and my health.

We faced three major obstacles. The first was the ocean's tide. While we were setting up our altar and arranging guest seating, the tide was coming in—not going out. Yep, we had to reset everything higher on the beach before heading off to get dressed. The second was the lack of a sound system. Air current from the tide washed all sound out, preventing our guests from hearing the service. The last thing we failed to take into consideration was my physical strength; even though I had gained freedom from full-time wheelchair use, I quickly tired. I had not regained enough strength to walk long distances in the sand.

Hawaiians blow three times into a conch shell to invite the holy trinity to their events. Because we didn't have a sound system, our guests could not hear the announcement of our arrival when we blew the conch shell. This activity became thirty attempts by six different people to make the horn loud enough. Our efforts seemed futile as we blew the shell in the direction of our guests, whose backs were facing us. I am not sure if they ever heard the shell horn. However, it was priceless watching our very serious attempts, which made our cheeks puff out like blowfish and our entire heads turn candy-apple red. We finally decided that either they had already heard it or it was not going to happen, so we proceeded along our sandy path towards the huppa.

Chip and I started the ceremony by placing one of the flower leis around each other's neck. We later sent these leis out to sea as an invitation to our deceased family and friends to join our celebration. For the lasso ceremony, Pastor Ron Wilson wrapped the lei in an infinity symbol around our wrists as he prayed a blessing over our reunion. We used this Hawaiian tradition to replace the exchange of rings since we were already wearing our rings.

The ceremony concluded with a very special tradition: the wreath ceremony. My friend Brenda prepared a beautiful floral wreath with fresh flowers on the outside and a little biodegradable shelf in the middle. The middle section was to hold tissue paper, on which we wrote past hurts and trials. Under normal circumstances, the little papers would be ignited and burst into flames as the wreath was sent out to sea. Fires on this beach were forbidden, however, so, instead, Chip threw the wreath as far as he could into the surf.

This particular tradition suited us, as it was our opportunity to write down every trial, fear, and hurt that we had experienced in the prior year. Hawaiian tradition says that when the wreath returns to the shore, those past hurts will be gone, permanently lifted away. How awesome to couple a wedding anniversary with a celebration of new life! It marked a specific time we could celebrate every year as the new start for our lives together.

In the reception hall, we named our tables for each of the Hawaiian Islands, and provided fun facts about each. Our servers were dressed in Hawaiian clothing instead of dress suits, and we had planned our menu as if we had just arrived for a Hawaiian luau on the beach. There were no worries, only happy times. In all, I could not have asked for a more fitting way to celebrate our lives' trials and victories. I felt so free and immensely blessed to do as much as I did. I consider that ceremony a liberation of sorts from the oppression I had felt during the prior months.

I stress the many intricate details invested in this celebration because it marked an end to one of the darkest periods in my life. It was as if every detail in the execution of this celebration provided one more drop in the bucket of healing for me. Each part of the ceremony gave me more strength and more motivation to use my experiences to help others. From this celebration forward, the pendulum clearly shifted.

Over the next several months, the swelling in my nerves continued to diminish, allowing many of my abilities to return completely. With each one, I could feel my heart changing for the better. Looking back, I cannot believe the kind of a person I had become before the diagnosis. All of my past flaws were coming to the light. My heart cried out in apology to every person I had ever wronged or hurt.

I started a personal journey, acknowledging and scrutinizing who I was becoming. Although this part of the journey could last indefinitely, it was time to apply the life lessons I had learned through my recent trials.

This is young
two-and-a-half
year-old me. In
the house I called
my castle.
(Left to right)
Gretchen, Jon,
my daddy.

This is four-and-a-
half year-old me. I
had already
developed a strong
opinion against my
mother by this
point.

These are pictures taken of me in the two years around when my parents were divorced. The time when I was so depressed that I tried to kill myself.

This photo was taken during a modeling photo shoot
my sophomore year in high school, 1988.

In the foreground, you see the empty muffin wrapper. Under
the table, you see my Zoey hiding. I said she looks like she put
herself in jail.

133

These were my little cherubs who protected me in my blindness by making grunting sounds when anyone approached me. One sat on either side of me. Mai Tai is in the front and her mommy, Zoey, is behind her.

These are the Hello Kitty stuffed animals. Survivor is on the left with the dinosaur and Kelekena is on the right with a white kitty.

This is the surf board I painted when I had no depth perception and I could not see color. My daughter handed me the colors when I asked for them.

Me working with sea turtles in Spring 2010.

Spring 2005, releasing my lamprey larvae (babies) back into the field. Pictured left to right, Dr. Gordon Weddle,

I was injecting the fish larvae into the substrate, where they live for several years.

I walked my first 5K race in 2009, two and a half years after the major M.S. issues. I completed it in one hour and twenty minutes. I walked behind the wheel chair but never sat in it. (Left to Right) Gretchen, David.

Two years later, spring 2011, I completed the same race as above in 45 minutes. (Left to Right) Chip, Gretchen.

My first 8K race. Space Walk of Fame April 9, 2011. I completed it in 1:25:15. I'm so happy to have finished.

This picture was taken at Omega hospital on the day of my discharge, March 2008. (Left to right) Dr. Sullivan, Gretchen, Chip.

Coming out of surgery March 5, 2008.

This was taken in New Orleans after my first surgery, March 2008. It was the night before driving back to Titusville. (Left to Right) Mark, Jan, Chip, Gretchen.

Our wedding ceremony December 1997. Left to right Gretchen, Cristi, Gretchen, Rana.

Pre-ceremony picture for our vow renewal in 2007.

Pre-ceremony pictures. This was the most walking I did without my wheel chair since the medical crisis struck. Walking was slow and at times supported by Chip.

2007 ceremony at a glance on left. The right is the lasso ceremony.

Me wearing my peacock colors for graduation from graduate school, spring 2013.

Graduation, spring 2013. (From left to Right) Brett, Gretchen, Ryan.

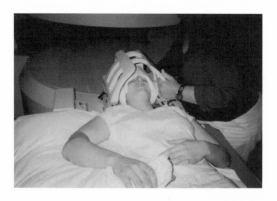

Me in the MRI, 2001. They were nice enough to let me take my ducky with me, seen in my right hand.

Me resting, during a study session, with my two little cherubs, Zoey and Lani, after a day at the infusion center, spring 2011.

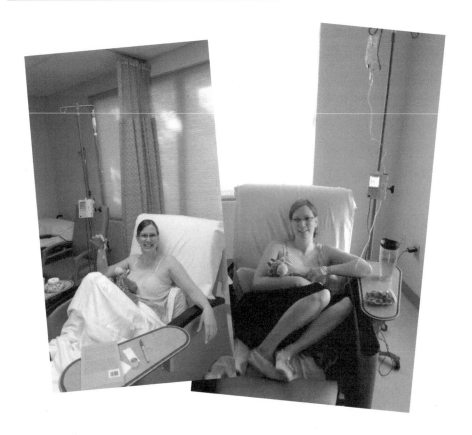

Above is my seat at the infusion center, September 2015.My nurse gave me a teeny tiny hand bell for when I needed something. That was the start to silliness for the week.

Above was taken on the last day for this round of steroids September 2015. Clearly, there are good days and not so good days. By this day, I was not feeling so good, that's a forced smile.

Me at the infusion center with my two nurses, summer 2014. (Left to right) Sylvia, Gretchen, Jeanine.

Zoey with her heart monitor on, February 2017.
She was such a little trooper with all the testing they had to do on her.

This picture was taken at the celebration of life for my dad in August 2014. (Left to right) Rana, Cristi, Gretchen, Kachina.

*Left*: May 29, 2010, celebrating our birthday together. I turned 37-years-old and Zoey turned 6-years-old. She was always my cuddle bug. *Center*: February 2017, saying Aloha – until later my angel. With leis from Hawaii, Chip and I went to the beach to let Zoey go by sending her lei out to sea. *Right*: February 2017, some loose Hawaiian flowers returned and looked like Zoey's foot prints in the sand.

Cristi and I with our daughters in August 2015.
(Left to right) Ashley, Gretchen, Cristi, and Sarah.

Wanda was taking pictures of my family on the river, 2013. We got one
with her too. (Left to right) Gretchen, Wanda.

# Chapter 12
# The Next Wave

I was awaiting results from a DNA blood test for the BRCA breast cancer gene[5], which runs in my mother's family, so I had a feeling the results were in when I saw the mail carrier. When I opened the mailbox and saw the envelope from the DNA lab, I felt the proverbial carpet under my feet yanked away. This left me feeling as if I was floating aimlessly, with no solid structure to ground me.

Chip was away for the weekend, and the lab results were in my hands. I knew in my gut what the results were going to reveal, but I didn't want to see them. I put the envelope on the counter and walked out of the room, then back in again. I stared at the envelope and tried to read through it, as if I had super powers. At last, I decided it was time to open the letter. As I read the results, I dropped to the floor and cried.

I had tested positive to the BRCA 2 gene, which is the gene responsible for both female and male breast cancers. I am sure I sobbed out of fear for my children's future as well as for my feeling of relief at finally knowing for certain, one way or the other. However, I now faced another trial.

---

[5] Breast cancer organization contact information is in Appendix B.

My relationship with my mother was already shattered, broken beyond measure. When I read the test results, I felt that wound reopen. For a minute. Then I immediately let it go because I knew I did not have the strength to handle my feelings. This latest legacy from my mother was not fair, but I had to forgive my mother or risk my powers to heal by holding a grudge against her.

My second thought was for my kids. "What about their futures?" I asked myself. I have one boy and one girl, but gender didn't matter with this gene; it affects both. Suddenly my mind rolled fast-forward, and I started blaming myself for what could happen to my children. The timing of this news was horrible because I still had two more days before Chip would return home. I needed his support.

The "poor me" frustration went full throttle as those thoughts and concerns continued to recycle through my brain. Why did the results have to be positive? Why did I have to get these results while Chip was away? Yet, admittedly, I had strongly suspected the positive results—although suspecting and knowing are two different things. I had been hanging on to the hope that I would evade that gene. Now that hope was gone, so I worried about my future. Why did I have to go through this after what I had been enduring for the past year? Besides, I was not yet fully healed! Fortunately, before I could verbally beat myself to death, Chip returned home.

I was able to sit down and talk to Chip about my fears that night. We debated whether this was the right timing for preventive surgery. We speculated about how it would go and where the best place was to have the procedure. Did I have other options? With a positive

BRCA breast cancer gene and a family history of aggressive breast cancer, I had a decision to make. Soon.

Honestly, the answer came easily. The right decision was to proceed with the prophylactic breast surgery. This gave me control over my future in a positive way, even though it was a little scary.

Once again, Chip was fantastic in the many ways he was supportive. All he wanted was for me to be comfortable with my decision and know that he could physically be there to support me. Once we made the decision, he helped me research locations, and he arranged for time off from work with his employer.

Now I had work to do: researching the right doctor to perform the prophylactic double mastectomy. This procedure removes healthy tissue in an effort to stave off the development of cancer. My intention was to find a doctor who would not only do the double mastectomy, but also the reconstruction. I knew I was too young not to opt for reconstruction. However, I didn't want implants because I thought there might be complications from MS that would cause my body to attack itself. I was hopeful that we could find a doctor willing to use my own tissue.

To reduce complications, I wanted to have the surgery near my home. However, I quickly learned that having the procedure done locally did not reduce complications. In fact, it added a level of frustration I did not want to deal with. One of the doctors I consulted told me I was too skinny and suggested implants. Another said he could do the surgery, but would have to cut muscle and relocate it with the fat to provide a blood supply. I did not want to do that.

If the muscle were inadequate, it would probably not be strong enough to recover from the surgery. If the tissue was good, I did not want doctors to damage it by cutting and moving it. One surgeon even suggested prosthetics. I thought, "Hello! I am thirty-four years old. What is that going to do to my self-esteem?" I refused to consider any of those options. Either I was going to give up on the search, or I had to search farther from home. Giving up was not an option.

One of my dad's friends had recently gone through a double mastectomy and reconstruction. The procedure she had undergone was experimental, but had an exceptional success rate.

Upon inquiry, my dad explained that his friend had undergone surgery at the Center for Restorative Breast Surgery in New Orleans.[6] When I contacted the center, they explained that the procedure would include the double mastectomy and reconstruction. For my body, they would use gluteal fat by moving tissue from my bum and applying it to my chest. The blood supply was going to come from arteries, not muscle. Because these procedures fulfilled my personal requirements for having the surgery, I scheduled surgery for March of 2008 at *The Center*.

By the end of 2007, my pending surgery was occupying my mind to the point of nearly rendering me functionless. I decided I should get a job to fill my time until I left for New Orleans. If all went well, I could come home to a job waiting for me. After filling out

---

[6] The Center for Restorative Breast Surgery information is in Appendix B.

several applications, I received an offer to become a hotel front-desk supervisor.

I have to back up in my story here. My mother-in-law, Ruth, was a restless person who found it difficult to stay in one place—which made it easy for her to follow her dreams of traveling. She had created a bucket list of all the things she wanted to do before she died. She told us she was preparing to cross one line item off her bucket list by moving to Alaska, but partway there, she decided to stay in Montana instead. Then, for some reason unknown to us, she decided to return to Florida in August of 2007. Since she had sold her Florida home before she left, she came to live with our family.

Five months after she arrived, she went to a cardiologist with complaints about being tired all the time. He told her that her defibrillator lead was not connected to her heart monitor, and that was causing the problem. He needed to replace the device so that when her heartbeats slowed, the monitor would keep her heart pumping. He scheduled her for surgery during the last week of January 2008.

As her surgery date neared, the more nervous she became. I heard her up at night pacing the floor and fidgeting in the kitchen by the open refrigerator. On those nights, I crawled out of bed, poured myself a drink, and sat with her. I knew my nerves were on edge, with my own surgery just under five weeks away, so I could only imagine how nervous she was, two days away from her surgery.

In those late hours, I believe we found peace by sharing our anxieties over our impending surgeries. She talked about her fear of the electrical lead that was dangling loose in her chest. She believed it could just zap her to her death at any minute. I talked about my fears dealing with the removal of such a deeply personal female area of my body. What would that do to my self-image? Because Ruth was Chip's mom, I opted not to discuss my concerns over what impact this would have on my husband's views of my body. I was deeply concerned about the impact this surgery would have on our intimate life and, ultimately, on our marriage.

I loved my talks with Ruth; they were deep, honest, and full of emotion. Sometimes women desperately need to make that kind of connection.

Ruth successfully made it to and through her surgery. Once she was on her way to recovery, I was the one on the surgical deck. As my nerves were twisting in knots late at night, Ruth returned the favor of getting out of bed to talk with me. We focused on the major differences between our situations.

First of all, I had to go out of state for my surgery. Some of my greatest apprehensions involved going into surgery with a surgeon I had never met, leaving my children at home for two weeks, and not having any supportive people with us in New Orleans. Ruth helped me talk through the necessary planning. On a fun note, she took the time to suggest some good restaurants to try in New Orleans because it was one of her favorite places to visit.

Many of my concerns were resolved before we left. My mother-in-law's job didn't allow her to become the sole caregiver for our kids during this time, so my dad and his fourth wife, Phyllis, flew in to take care of the kids for the two weeks we would be away. In addition, Chip and I were part of an Emmaus community within our church. It was through this group that we gained support during the surgery. Our local Emmaus community contacted the Emmaus community in New Orleans on our behalf.

On a March day in 2008, we began the drive to Louisiana. Stress about the surgery itself was minimal, primarily because I fully believed my God was in control. I still had apprehensions over what my doctor would be like and how badly the procedure would hurt, but the trip to New Orleans helped to distract me from my apprehensions. Chip and I used the drive as an opportunity to discuss how we could turn this trip into a vacation, since we had never been there before. Of course, while we were in town, in Ruth's honor, we took time to visit a couple of the restaurants she had suggested.

When we arrived, the streets were still busy with Marti Gras traffic, talk, laughter, and activities. The traditional Mardi Gras colors—purple, green, and gold—were everywhere, and people were still exchanging beads. Our accommodations were in the restored eighteenth-century French Quarter, at the Place D'Armes.

Several buildings made up the configuration of this hotel. Of the different buildings, we stayed in the part that was once a children's home. According to the check-in clerk, this building was featured on the city's haunted tour. She shared with us that hotel patrons in the past had told her about a little boy who played with his ball up and down the hallway. I very much enjoyed hearing so many details of the area's rich history, but my looming pre-surgical activities were fighting for my conscious thought space. Thankfully, I was mentally able to soak in my surroundings.

First thing in the morning, *The Center* sent a limousine to transport Chip and me to Omega Hospital, where I met with my surgeon for the first time. I had knots in my stomach and felt vulnerable when the doctor asked me to disrobe. Of course, I was there for a double mastectomy and reconstruction using tissue from my tail end. How would he be able to do that without first seeing the parts?

To break my tension, I jokingly suggested that he insert squeaky toys during the surgery. "It will be funny to watch responses when people come in for a hug and hear a squeak," I chuckled. My suggestion was successful at lightening the mood in the room for Chip and me. It even made for further humorous conversation in the room between us all. This was exactly what I needed to calm me down.

Once I disrobed, Dr. Sullivan began drawing surgical lines on me as if I was the canvas for his masterpiece—in truth, I was exactly that. Though I felt uncomfortable about this part of the procedure, the doctor and his staff were fabulous at helping me feel as comfortable as possible under the circumstances. In fact, I felt quite pampered, like royalty.

After my appointment with the reconstruction surgeon, I went upstairs to meet with the oncologist who was responsible for the double mastectomy. He talked to me about what it meant to test positive for the BRCA 2 breast cancer gene. Before this appointment, I did not know that the BRCA gene had a connection to ovarian cancer. Because several family members had occurrences of ovarian cancer, I opted to have my ovaries removed as well as my breasts. However, that procedure would not take place during this stage of surgery, he told us.

After this meeting ended, we pre-registered for the next morning's surgery. Then the limousine returned us to the hotel.

The knots in my stomach resurfaced and tightened, making eating difficult. However, Chip and I still took time to walk around a few blocks, to see the area. While we strolled through the town, it was fascinating to learn that a movie company was filming a horror flick several blocks from where we were staying. When we returned to our hotel room, we prepared everything for the following morning, and then went to bed.

I could not sleep. Too many thoughts circled through my head. I was grateful for the awesome doctor and facilities. I was grateful for the warm and wonderful way the medical staff had treated both Chip and me. Then I started worrying that I would sleep through my alarm clock. I certainly did not want to miss this surgery. Yes, I seriously thought that!

Just as I started to doze off, I heard people talking outside the window. I realized they were part of a ghost tour in process, so I listened in. The tour guide was just outside my window, telling the story of my building. If you were not familiar with this hotel, you would not know from the exterior that you were standing in front of a guest room. I decided it might be fun to start playing with the blinds and lights. One person noticed and poked the person next to her, pointing at my window. For a few minutes, my antics got my mind off my insomnia. When the tourists left, I went back to bed and soon fell asleep.

The morning came early, and I was extremely tired. However, I was not worried about the lost sleep, because I knew I would be under anesthesia for several hours during surgery. The limousine picked us up at the hotel at 5:30 that morning, in order to get me to the hospital before 6:30.

Shortly after we arrived at the hospital, a pastor came into my room to pray with me. Pastor Jim had given us his contact information and suggested we connect with him when we arrived in New Orleans. Thanks to his visit, I felt a sense of peace and, oddly, excitement about going under the knife.

Walking down the hallway to the pre-op room, I had a vision of myself as a cow corralled for the slaughterhouse. That silly feeling did not last long, though, because the nurses and anesthetists immediately came in and began pre-surgical preparations. They asked a series of questions, took my vital signs, and started my IV. I had not processed that it was time for the surgery until they started wheeling me down the hallway to the operating room.

One of my greatest concerns involving this surgery was the considerable amount of time that Chip would be by himself while I was under anesthesia. I wanted nothing more than for him to have someone to sit with and help preoccupy his mind. He is not comfortable in crowds, so I hoped for smaller connections that were more intimate.

That is exactly what he got when three men from a New Orleans Emmaus community arrived and offered to sit with Chip. One of them, Mark Bugg, stayed for the entire nine-and-a-half-hour surgery, and was there to meet me when I woke up. Later that night, he returned with his wife, Jan, to introduce her to us.

The amount of love this couple showered on us was nothing short of divine. I imagine that after talking with someone for nine-and-a-half straight hours, as Mark did with Chip, you can no longer say you are strangers. You become more like family.

This couple exuded a selflessness I rarely see. They were in the middle of their honeymoon when they opted to come and be our support team. They lavished immense love upon us, a couple they had just met. We quickly developed a deep and intimate connection that no words can articulate. I loved appreciating how we were so well taken care of by this fabulous couple.

Before going under anesthesia, I made a passionate request not to have narcotics; I do not like the control they take away from me. Then I said good night and the lights went out for me. It felt like only minutes had passed before I opened my eyes again, although it was actually more than nine-and-a-half hours. Within minutes of coming off anesthesia, I woke up chattering incessantly with anyone who would listen—and some who would not. I think I even talked to my twin brother on the phone.

After waking up, my biggest complaint was dry mouth. The Sahara Desert dryness led to jokes about how much alcohol the doctors had given me to induce that case of cottonmouth. When I talked, it felt as if I was spitting talcum powder. My tongue could not move freely, which prevented proper enunciation. I became moderately annoyed that my speech was slurred so badly that people couldn't understand me. Yes, I was a hot mess, but a happy one. Literally, every other word ended with a sip of water.

Once the procedure was complete, I had a checklist of activities to follow for proper healing to take place. The textbook version allotted a certain amount of time post-surgery for each milestone. Within four hours, I had surpassed the checkmarks for the first day-and-a half. The list included such things as managing pain, being active, drinking enough, and emptying my bladder. After quickly attaining those milestones, the doctors removed both my catheter and IV, giving me liberty and freedom to move about the unit.

Chip was a trooper, as I knew he would be, of course. He woke up as often as I did. He reminded me of a mother who sleeps with one eye open. Every time I moved or whimpered, he jumped to make sure he could give me what I needed. Every hour on the hour, he helped me unhook my leg pumps so I could walk a few laps around the hospital unit. The first time I took a stroll, I felt as if my insides were going to drop out of my rear end. However, it was difficult to keep focus on my rear end. For the first time in my life, I couldn't see my feet because something that felt like elephants had been glued to my chest. This was definitely an augmentation baby.

The entire situation was quite surreal: going to sleep with breasts and waking up with breasts that had multiplied in size. They were so large that I felt they arrived at my destination five minutes before I did. Ahh, the thrills of swelling.

Twenty-four hours after the surgery, walking became much easier for me, accompanied by only minimal discomfort. I honestly felt good and didn't need much more than a strong dose of Motrin for my pain; I attribute the regular walking to this successful progression of healing.

I saw my oncologist on the second night, during one of my late-night walks. He looked at me and said, "I was told I had a patient who was wearing down my carpets. That must be you." He was not the only one who remarked about the frequency of my walking. I am a firm believer that exercise releases endorphins to help reduce pain and speed the healing process.

To help post-surgical healing, my neurologist told me not to take my MS injections for two weeks before the surgery and two weeks afterwards. I admit a level of concern crossed my mind about how my body would respond to the trauma of surgery. I was pleasantly surprised to see that my only neurologic symptom was tingling in my skin. That symptom quickly diminished when I got up to walk.

Care at the hospital was superb. The staff offered exceptional treatment and services, both to Chip and me. They always greeted us with smiles and sincere concern for how I was feeling—and Chip, too, for that matter. The room was like a high-class hotel, complete with a Murphy bed for Chip, a television, a microwave, and refrigerator. We both ate exceptional food; all meals were prepared off the hospital grounds and catered. To date I can say this was one of the best experiences in my life, something that most people cannot comprehend when talking about such a long and potentially traumatic surgery.

We remained in New Orleans for ten days, including our arrival a day early so we could enjoy the Mardi Gras festivities on the streets.

The second day was full of pre-operative visits. Day three covered the surgery. Then seven days of recovery followed.

*The Center* spoiled me by carting me around town in limousines, with a chauffeur who opened the doors while helping me in and out and treated me with such sensitivity. Chip and I were able to experience New Orleans for the first time, and we gained a new lifelong friendship (family-ship) with a super-fantabulous couple. No doubt, this couple was a silver lining for both Chip and me.

Before my discharge, my doctor removed the drains from under my breasts. However, when I went home, I still had two drains in my hips. On the drive home, I kept telling Chip I felt like I was a birdie on a wire. That was because the drains went through the sides of my hips and ran parallel with the incisions under the skin in my bum. In this way, when I was in the seated position, I felt as if I was sitting on skinny tubes.

When I am asked if I would undergo the surgery again, I say, "Yes, without a doubt—as long as it is at Omega Hospital with the team of doctors and staff from *The Center*. Collectively, they were significant silver linings for both Chip and me. The gray cloud that had hung over my head for ten years, dangling the threat of breast cancer, was now gone.

# Chapter 13
# Bonding Through Bandages

Ruth had her first surgery in mid-February of 2008. Chip and I left for New Orleans the first week in March, unfortunately, just at that time Ruth started to develop an infection at her surgical site. The antibiotics her doctor prescribed were unsuccessful in preventing a deeper infection. He scheduled her for a second surgery, to remove the entire defibrillator device.

Two weeks after I returned from my surgery, Ruth and I resumed our late-night talks to help her deal with her nerves. An amazing number of topics can come up when someone is scared about something. These talks made it possible for us to laugh through our tensions.

Ruth came home from the hospital with an open wound because the doctor wanted it to heal from the inside out. He said this would help reduce the risk of redeveloping infection. Initially, a home-health nurse came to our home to change her dressings, but the goal was for me to take over that role. The nurse demonstrated how to apply the wet/dry dressing change and told me I needed to do this three times a day. She would return every other day to check on the progress.

My time as a nurse in the 1990's, coupled with all my premedical coursework from the early 2000's, offered me in-depth experience with this type of wound care. This significantly helped Ruth's wound to heal much faster than her doctor and nurse had anticipated.

Call it shared fears or bonding time, but either way, our individual circumstances made my mother-in-law and me the optimum cohorts for planning individual responses to our surgeries. We were both in the active healing process simultaneously. I still had my hip drains and she had a deep open hole in her chest. In our time together during wound care, we shared our worries and vulnerabilities in a safe zone, knowing it was judgment-free. We talked about our goals for the future and the things that made us happy, sad, and hopeful. We shared fears over our surgical experiences and the hopes we had for the outcomes.

Changing Ruth's dressing became an art of dance. At first she looked away, so she did not see the hole in her chest—which had become a source of nightmares for her. In the nightmares, she could see her heart beating from the open hole. I was not afraid of hurting her because the post-surgical area was still numb, a side effect from surgery. The issue was the number of times I inadvertently caught my own post-surgical hip drains on objects, which caused me sharp pain.

When Ruth realized I was hurting myself, our picture changed to a picture of selfless love. She held my drains, allowing me to focus all of my attention on her wound care. Additionally, through her act of love, she redirected her attention from the hole in her chest to my drains. We had a crazy kind of symbiotic relationship that led to her doctor expressing amazement over how quickly she had fully healed.

The worst part about Ruth's situation was that without the defibrillator in her chest, she had to wear an external device. She despised it and called it her "annoying baby." The silly contraption had a habit of making a loud siren noise when it was not correctly in place, usually while she was sleeping or in the shower. I hoped for a speedy resolve because I did not think she deserved the hell she was experiencing.

As her chest incision was closing, but before the removal of my hip drains, Ruth and I decided it was time to go "paint the town". We shared a deep affinity for the same band, the Beach Boys, and when we heard they were coming to the Cocoa Beach Pier, we promised ourselves that no medical situation was going to keep us away. Unfortunately, we did not fully think out how far we had to walk after parking.

We must have been a pathetic sight to watch as we waddled down the beach very slowly, with what felt like rubber legs. Half the time she was holding me up and the other half of the time, I was holding her up. We were giggling like schoolgirls as we stumbled and swayed across the sand. Ruth was sporting her external contraption and my drains looked like clappers protruding from my hips.

We made it to the concert, but did not have tickets, so we sat outside the fence with other people in our same position – ticketless. Our outing was truly an accomplishment. We sat, talked, and listened to a few songs. When we caught our breath, we agreed that, though we really wanted to stay, we were completely worn out and should probably go home.

No words can describe how fortunate I was to experience this as my first-ever mother-daughter getaway. I felt like these moments were filling the void left by my mother's absence in my life.

Two-and-a-half months after the first surgery, I was contemplating round two of my mastectomy, the reconstruction phase. The very thought of this stage greatly overwhelmed me. I had just celebrated my thirty-fifth birthday, too young for a hysterectomy. Yet this surgery would include a complete hysterectomy, removing my ovaries, fallopian tubes, uterus, and cervix. I was desperate for a mommy to reassure me, and went to Ruth. I spent countless hours talking to her. Never-ending rounds of questions arose about a subject that was awkward to discuss.

I wondered whether the lack of hormone-producing glands would make me grow facial hair and develop a deep voice. Would my husband still find me attractive? How would the surgery affect our intimacy? I worried that I was about to become an "it" at the age of thirty-five—and that thought made me anxious. Ruthie continually reassured me that everything was going to be okay. In fact, she predicted that things would be much better after this surgery—and, to a great extent, she was right. The "much better" part she was referring to was the fact that I would no longer have the annoyance of a monthly female cycle. She also predicted that my massive mood swings would disappear.

Fortunately, none of my fears became a reality. But her predictions did.

The beginning of June rolled around all too fast. Before I knew it, Chip and I were packing and heading down the road on our return trip to New Orleans for round two: the hysterectomy and stage two of breast reconstruction.

Phoebe Walker

# Chapter 14
# Round Two in NOLA

To enjoy New Orleans with new experiences, we made reservations at a different hotel. However, my gut did not feel settled. I am not sure if it was claustrophobia due to the low ceilings of the old hotel or something else. Regardless, I was too uncomfortable to stay there. Chip took me to another hotel, where more issues of the same kind arose—coupled this time with much more street and hotel noise. I was already anxious about the pending surgery and just wanted calm and quiet. Fortunately, as we stood at the check-in counter, we received a phone call from Mark and Jan Bugg, the couple who had interrupted their honeymoon to help us during my first surgery in March.

The New Orleans Emmaus community was the conduit for our connection with the Buggs. They were middle-aged grandparents who, in my estimation, rank right up with the living angels who surrounded me during my blind invalid stage. Rarely do we cross paths with people who are as genuinely selfless as these individuals are. When Mark and Jan heard about our issues at the hotel, they graciously opened their home to us. We gratefully accepted.

In my mind, this trip to New Orleans had a gunmetal gray overcast from the start. Many aspects about it were different. First, the problems we had with two different hotels. Then we learned that we could not register for surgery at Omega Hospital because of my insurance. Instead, I had to register at a public hospital. Immediately, found myself becoming more negative and nervous about this experience.

My pre-surgery appointment at *The Center* was the lift-me-up I needed. The staff always seemed to know the right thing to say. The doctors, nurses, and administrators were fabulous and sensitive to the ways their patients were feeling. They continued treating me like royalty and doing what they could to ensure my comfort during all of the pre-surgical appointments.

On the day of surgery, I arrived at the hospital early, expecting the procedure to be much shorter than the first one. This time we did not request a pastoral visit. Mark Bugg was the only person at the hospital with us before I went under anesthesia. Once again, he was a silver lining for Chip, as they sat together through the entire surgery. Although we expected the procedure to take about four-and-a-half hours, complications occurred during the hysterectomy.

About the fifth hour into the surgery, thirty minutes after it should have been complete, a hospital chaplain walked into the waiting area, sat at a desk, and made a call enquiring which family he needed to talk to about a patient who had just died during surgery. Chip told me that when he heard those words he thought his heart stopped beating and dropped to the floor. He decided that the patient in question was me, and that was the reason why no one had been out to talk to him about my surgery. When the chaplain walked into another waiting room, to talk to the family there, Chip realized he was actually breathing. Only then could he compose himself.

Several years later, when we told my dad about this incident, he chuckled in sympathy. As a former hospital chaplain, my dad knew it was the responsibility of the doctor to inform families of a death. The chaplain would go in afterwards, to help the family with the next steps.

After about eight-and-a-half hours of surgery, I was moved to the recovery room. Coming out of this surgery was more difficult than the first. When I woke up, I heard someone say, "Don't roll over. You just had surgery." That brought me into the present, where I realized I was not only in pain, but the pain was so intense it felt as if circus animals had mauled me. In my half-conscious state, I asked the nurse for pain medication. As soon as she injected it into the IV, I felt instant euphoria, followed by, "Lights out, man." I was knocked out cold.

It seemed like only a moment later when my head popped up and I asked for more medicine. The third time I awoke was different. I still had pain, but I did not ask for more medication. This was good timing, because my regular hospital room was ready and my nurse joked that she was getting stingy with the painkillers, saying that she would not let me have any more. That was okay. I honestly did not hurt enough to take more. I simply enjoyed giving her a hard time about refusing to give a patient pain medicine.

In my room, I tried sitting up for the first time. BIG mistake! When I sat up, I must have triggered my sneeze button. Did that hurt! After my sneezing fit, I didn't think I had any innards left. I was certain the pressure of my sneezing must have forced them out to where they were covering the walls, floor, and ceiling. Maybe I should have just stayed lying down because there was not a part of my torso that didn't feel full of holes.

But the situation worsened. A nurse told me I needed to start coughing. She handed me a pillow to support my abdomen and reduce the pain while I coughed. She was funny. Of course, I told her "NO." Besides, I didn't think I had anything left inside to cough out after that sneeze. She giggled and explained that it was for my own good, to keep my lungs clear. "That will assist with healing," she promised.

Half-dazed by heavy coughing into the pillow, something hit me with absolute certainty, though the timing was not optimal. I had an overwhelming conviction that I should instigate a breast-cancer awareness conference to share what I learned through my process. Then I began questioning my abilities to speak publicly as well as produce a full program capable of holding an audience's attention.

Fortunately, as quickly as the thought entered my mind, I put it on hold, because the surgeon who performed my hysterectomy came into my room. She shared surgical details that explained my immense pain and the extra time under anesthesia. Apparently, during the hysterectomy, she identified a case of endometriosis that took several hours to clean out.

My stay at this hospital was not as pleasant as my stay at Omega. I just wanted to leave. Therefore, I did everything I could to gain a speedy discharge. When I left the hospital the next day, we returned to our friends' home. From a recovery standpoint, that was the worst day. The pain was so intense on every side of my body that I fell to my knees, with my arms crossed on a chair in front of me. I placed my head on my arms as I wailed out for mercy. Chip contacted my surgeons at Omega, who called in a narcotic pain medication to the pharmacy. That night I took one pill and fell asleep. The next day I felt much better and was able to get up and become more active, using only Motrin for pain.

On the seventh day post-op, we went to follow-up appointments at *The Center* and the gyn-oncological surgeon. After both gave us the okay, we started our twelve-hour trip back home. This drive was so horribly uncomfortable that when we stopped for lunch, I wanted to shop for a pillow to cushion my abdomen. While we were eating lunch, I saw a Build-A-Bear workshop out the window. Like a nagging child, I begged Chip to let me go in and make an animal instead of buying a pillow. He agreed.

We had just walked out of the Build-A-Bear workshop and were walking through the parking lot when our kids called. They said a package had arrived from UPS. I told them they could open it and tell me what was inside. Rana had sent me a Build-A-Bear animal! I thought she knew me well, but I didn't realize how well until this gift. Believe it or not, she sent the exact same animal with the exact same outfit that I had just purchased for myself: Hello Kitty with the Hawaiian outfit. Funny, I am not much of a Hello Kitty person, but I do love anything tropical. Kelekena was the name she gave the kitty she made because that is my name in Hawaiian. I named mine Survivor because that is how I felt.

⁓

At home, I began planning the breast-cancer awareness conference. I decided on a date in October, Breast Cancer Awareness Month. Next, I needed a location. My church was always busy with a plethora of activities, and one of its primary missions is mothers of preschoolers. Since this was the perfect age group for my conference audience, I decided this should be the venue. I sought permission and then I looked for speakers. I collected educational materials to hand out and created a power point presentation. Lastly, to entice attendance for such a heavy topic on a weekend when people could be outdoors enjoying themselves, I ran around town collecting door prizes, predominantly from spas.

The conference ran perfectly. Three speakers, including myself, spoke to thirty women for more than two hours, which included a question-and-answer session and time for the raffle drawings. The audience was the perfect size, not too large or too small. We had more than enough literature to go around, and people had opportunities to have their questions answered. It was a good feeling at the end to hear comments like "I didn't know that before now" and "Now I have information to chew on before making a decision about my procedure." I went into the event believing I would be happy if I reached just one person. Coming out of the event, I was grateful to have reached several.

Through this life event, I identified a need and my capabilities to fill that need. My hardships were turning into blessings. From this, I knew I had to devote more time to sharing my experiences and knowledge with other people.

Phoebe Walker

# Chapter 15
# An Angel Called Ruth

My friend Wanda lives six houses up the road from me. We met in the spring 1998, when she and her family moved into base housing in Jacksonville, two doors down from my house. Through the many military moves both of us made over the years, we maintained our friendship. Then, when Chip and I had our vow renewal service in the spring of 2007, I invited her to be a bridesmaid. She flew in from Hawaii and fell in love with my new house. When she learned that the model home was across the street, she went to check it out. Wanda was so impressed that she decided to have a house built for her down the road from me. Before she flew back to Hawaii, she signed a contract for that lot and the construction. Then I welcomed Wanda and her family into that house in fall 2007.

Two weeks after the breast cancer conference in October 2008, I found the quickest way to get a Kirby sales person out of your house: receive an alarming phone call.

Wanda and I both had a Kirby sales representative in our homes on that particular day. Throughout their sales pitch, we were texting each other to see which of us would finish first and who would be first to receive the free bottle of soda they had offered. The poor man at my house was right in the middle of a demonstration—he had just put carpet shampoo on a large area of carpet in my family room— when the phone rang. Because it was an unknown number, I tossed the phone to TJ. He immediately passed it back to me, saying the person insisted on talking to me. I could not hear over the vacuum, so I walked into the kitchen to take the call.

I didn't know the out-of-state area code on the caller ID and did not recognize the woman's voice on the phone. She said, "I'm not at home. I'm in North Carolina. Your mom is at my house, and she's dead."

My jaw dropped and I fell to the floor in shock while I tried to register what she had just said. In my confusion, I thought, "How can this be?" I didn't understand who the woman was, but I knew Ruth was not in North Carolina. She was working as a CNA with home healthcare. "Are you calling the right phone number?" I asked, my heart pounding furiously. After asking the woman on the phone several questions, I finally established that she was one of Ruth's patients and she was visiting someone in North Carolina. She explained that my mother-in-law, who lived here in Florida, had offered to stay her house to care for her dogs. Then I remembered Ruth saying she would be dog sitting when she left our house.

Ruth's patient lived with another woman. When this woman heard the patient's dogs barking persistently from inside the bedroom, she went to investigate. She opened the door to the room where Ruth was staying and found Ruth lying facedown on the bed. The woman called 911. When the EMTs arrived, they pronounced Ruth "expired". Because Ruth had been living with us, ours was the only number the patient had to contact in an emergency.

Chip and I scurried around our house to grab what we needed before heading to the patient's house, where we found Ruth's body and the detectives.

Since we were the first family members contacted, I grabbed the phone book and made calls while Chip drove us to the address we'd been given. I called Ruth's mother, one of her sisters, and Chip's two younger brothers. We spent several hours trying to contact Chip's sister, because she was out of the country.

Meanwhile, our daughter Ashley, who had just turned eleven years old, was attending the fall school social with friends, and we knew she would remain there for hours. We left our fourteen-year-old son at the house to help the Kirby sales representative clean up and get out. This same night, we were supposed to put a large Hawaiian salad together for TJ's Junior ROTC luau fundraiser. Unfortunately for TJ, this was also something we had to impose upon him. We had mountains of salad materials and dishes that he needed to give to the Junior ROTC parent who agreed to come to our house to pick them up.

A police investigator led us into the room to see Ruth's body. We gave him positive identification. Judging by her position, she must have been sitting on the side of the bed going through papers when she died. She appeared to have fallen sideways, with her hand over her heart. When I saw this, I fell to my knees next to Ruth and began to cry. I put my hand on her head and could feel her skin was still warm. From a medical standpoint, I remembered that the sense of hearing is supposed to be the last thing to go. With the hope that she could still hear me, I told her that I loved her so much and while I would miss her, it was okay to go home.

Chip was very upset about the loss of his mother, but he did not respond the same way I did, which was with endless tears. I didn't want to leave the side of Ruth's lifeless body, but Chip felt very uncomfortable there. He opted to walk in to identify her and then he walked right back out of the room. All he wanted to do was see the body and make sure it was really her. As the oldest sibling, he turned his attention to the duties of executor of his mother's estate. He wanted to make sure her end-of-life affairs were in order and that each sibling was taken care of.

This loss of my mother-in-law was very difficult for me, although I was grateful that she was no longer in physical pain. I had been a part of my husband's family for nearly thirteen years when Ruth died. I watched her emotional heart change for the better in the prior two years, and I felt fortunate to have had her living in our home for the last fourteen months of her life. Months prior to this day, she started having a thirst to reconnect with her family and redevelop relationships. Until this point, she always said she preferred relationships with animals to those with people.

While she lived with us, we became accustomed to eating meals together at the dinner table, walking together, playing board games and lottery scratch-offs, and watching movies. One of the movies we talked about in depth was *The Bucket List*. We discussed our bucket lists. Ruth loved to travel and announced that although she never did make it to Alaska, after traveling to Montana, she decided she could cross Alaska off her list; she didn't want to go there anymore. The incomplete part of her bucket list included a trip to Spain to visit her daughter and a move to Greenland. However, shortly before she died, she decided that she would miss her family too much to go to Greenland.

Most of us remember Ruthie as someone who did her laundry with her pockets full. One day, a pen from Ruth's laundry exploded and stained one of Ashley's dresses. Ruth felt horrible about it and wanted to make things right for Ashley. The three of us went shopping for a new dress. We enjoyed talking through dressing room walls as if no one else was there. Until this point, Ashley and I had not experienced this kind of generational connection with family.

Ruth and I bonded the most during 2008, in the midst of our multiple surgical procedures. Her first one was in January and mine was in March. Her second surgery was in April, and mine was in June. With both of us requiring six weeks of recovery after each surgery, you can see where we overlapped. We found the experiences much easier to go through because we had each other to share pain, stories, and medical gauze for dressings. We made a great team through these healing processes.

Ruth was more than a mother figure to me. She was also a friend. I was thankful for the late-night talks we had, no matter who was doing the leaning and who was doing the listening. I enjoyed her funny antics and our fun time out on the town, whether alone or with my friends. I appreciated the feedback that she gave when I was working on projects and how instrumental she was as a grandmother. I remember all the stories she shared with the kids. Through our many activities together, I grew so used to her living with us that I really missed her when she was gone.

The kids fondly remember their grandmother. They say they are still amazed at how they could hear her sawing logs through two shut doors; her snoring was legendary in the house. Ashley said she was glad she finally figured out where her shampoo was going: Ruth was using it. Moreover, both TJ and Ashley still laugh as they remember how Ruth was immensely technology-challenged. She continually locked herself out of all her favorite shows by setting the parent controls to "G"-rated programs only.

Ruth made me think, laugh, cry, and want to love even more. To me, she will always be a wonderful, beautiful woman. I have a void without her that no one can fill. Certainly, she was a significant silver lining in my life, particularly during her last months with us.

# Chapter 16
# Sisters

After I returned from surgery in June 2008, I quit my job. By October, I wished I still had that job as a distraction, to redirect my attention from the loss of Ruth. Just as I was completing all the technical work on Ruth's financials, I put my focus on studying for the Graduate Record Exam (GRE).

My desire to return to college goes back far, to the days when I moved in with my dad and realized how much I enjoyed learning. That was when I decided I would never stop working on continuing education.

Flash forward to present day, and education became an excellent distraction from this disease that I live with. When I succeeded in class, it helped me forget the things the disease made difficult for me to accomplish.

When I started working for the hotel at the end of 2007 and into 2008, I met a woman named Robin Rich. She was a night auditor who put in her two weeks' notice during my first week on the job because, she said, she was engaged and planned to move out of state. Robin and I shared only a professional relationship. I knew she was a good worker. On a personal level, however, she used to mock my faith. Heavily. That didn't bother me too much, however, because I knew she only had a few more days working for me.

Almost a year and a half later, in the fall of 2009, Chip and I joined a discipleship class at our church, where I was surprised to see Robin. She had been assigned to our small group. She had not married after all, so after a brief time away, she returned to town. In spite of all the grief she had given me about my faith, I discovered that she had a strong desire to develop her own faith.

In our group, she was the one who flourished the most. Just like a sponge, she absorbed every detail of our lessons. She asked many questions and took detailed notes that filled every available white space in her workbook—including spaces between lines. When looking in her book, it was difficult to determine whether or not the published words outnumbered those she wrote by hand.

As our class progressed, I felt called to sponsor her for a Walk to Emmaus Weekend in November 2009. Robin had an immense desire to learn more than it appeared our class could offer her, and a weekend to Emmaus could fill that spiritual need.

As a rule, those who serve on an Emmaus weekend cannot also sponsor someone for that weekend. In this way, the individual (pilgrim) will have the sponsor's undivided attention during that time. I was serving the November walk, but I was also sponsoring Robin. I was overjoyed to receive special permission to do both. However, I had one condition: I had to find a co-sponsor.

I searched for and found someone willing to co-sponsor Robin with me. It was Joy Lesky. This fantastic woman was part of a clown ministry that brought joy to those who were feeling down, to those who were celebrating, and everyone in between. In fact, she was one of the first people to sit with me during the administration of my IV medication at the infusion center. I always felt like a queen when she offered foods that would help calm my stomach from the medicine. She also massaged my feet to help me relax while I received the IV. I was excited that she was willing to team up with me again, this time to co-sponsor Robin.

Robin suffered a great deal from spinal stenosis, a condition where vertebras constrict the spinal cord, creating intense pain most of the time. Regardless of the pain, she attended the weekend and did the best she could to remain as active as possible. In fact, while she was there, she participated by writing many poems and songs. It was fascinating how she could sit down and pour them out in less than five minutes without making changes throughout the writing process.[7]

On this same weekend in November of 2009, I met another woman who would become a very dear friend of mine, a woman who oftentimes serves as a stand-in mommy. Her name is Jackie Haines.

---

[7] Robin's poetry, Appendix C

She is even more petite than I am and has a metabolism that needs no steroids to produce high energy and enthusiasm. Her personality is a powerhouse of excitement and abundant love for her neighbor. It was on this weekend that I learned her husband had passed away almost exactly two weeks after Ruth died, in 2008.

Our connection seemed natural from the beginning. We felt as if we had been life-long friends from the moment we met. The weekend deeply impressed Jackie and renewed her faith. The connection was so profound that before she left the camp, she signed up to serve the next Emmaus weekend, in the spring of 2010. After returning home, Jackie, Robin, and I started regular weekly accountability meetings that drew us even closer.

The culmination of our meetings created the platform for the next stage of my life. My accountability group was a permanent silver lining that walked me through a significant transitional stage in my life. Through our continued meetings, I gained the strength and encouragement to dive into life with absolute abandon of self, while fully relying on my faith.

# Chapter 17
# The Call

For as long as I can remember, I have wanted to become a doctor. In fact, after I completed my associate of arts degree in Nebraska in the summer of 2001, I was accepted at the University of North Carolina at Chapel Hill for the pre-medical program. When my neurological issues began developing that fall, I decided to decline my acceptance. It was a very difficult decision, to turn down the opportunity to prepare for going on to medical school. I felt defeated. The survivor in me said that even though I was not going to pursue my first dream, I could stay in the discipline and still make a difference in the field of biology. I went on to complete my undergraduate studies in 2005, with a Bachelor of Science degree in biology and a minor in environmental science.

We settled into our forever home in Titusville and my health became stabilized in 2008. At that time, I started researching universities and programs. I was excited to learn about a conservation biology doctoral program at the University of Central Florida (UCF). The UCF biology department offered a sea turtle program that fascinated me. I worked diligently to get admitted into that department.

After multiple attempts in 2009, I was finally able to meet with the advisor for the sea turtle project, and we discussed opportunities for joining the team. During the visit, I felt obligated to discuss my medical condition. I explained how one of my worst enemies was too much direct heat, but that I had assistive devices to keep me cool. From the beginning, I was open and honest about my disability and my plan to keep it controlled.

To make sure I was physically capable of doing the work, I met with the sea turtle team on several occasions. I felt as if the sky opened and doused me with blessings every time they let me accompany them in the boats to collect data. I remember thinking to myself, "This is what it must feel like to be the recipient of Make-a-Wish Foundation." The blessing was so grand. I know I was beaming every day when I went out on the boats to survey the turtles. Afterwards. I always returned home with the sensation that my legs were still wobbling from standing in the boat for so long. Even so, I jumped up, punched the air, and shouted, "WAHOOOOOOOOOOOOOOOOOOIE! This was the best day yet!"

I do not deny the physical strain of the work, having to keep balanced while lifting the turtles onto the boat, taking measurements, and tagging them, sometimes in turbulent waters. However, this physical requirement can be difficult for anyone, with or without a disease. If I could have made a full-time job working with the sea turtles, it would have been the perfect job for me. Bottom line, I cannot thank "Doc", Dr. Llewellyn Ehrhart, enough for giving me this "opportunity of a lifetime". After each day I was in the field, I shed tears of joy for this amazing silver lining.

In March of 2010, Jackie, Robin, and I went back to serve on an Emmaus team, and I sponsored Wanda. This weekend was unique in a way that I cannot fully articulate. What I can tell you is that it created the foundation for my next walk in life.

Yet something was peculiar about the weekend, and the sensation lingered after I arrived home. When we pulled into the driveway, the front of my house looked very different. It was dark and hazy—like a scary movie. I traced around windows, doors, and flowerbeds with my eyes. Nothing was different. When I went inside, the lights were dim, and the same phenomenon occurred. Now, that was odd. I thought. How did the inside of my house get hazy?

My surroundings remained hazy as I unpacked. Before I knew it, for no reason, I was crying. Horrible thoughts circled in my head: "You're too fat and ugly." "You're diseased." "How are you ever going to finish a degree?" "You're going to go back to school? You'll get halfway through it and not be able to finish." "You'll be taking your family's money and flushing it down the toilet." and, "You're not good enough to do anything." That night, I cried myself to sleep.

No one in my family approached me during this time. In fact, it was so confusing to me. I never could articulate the details to them. I just needed to trust that I was emotionally where I needed to be and that I would be guided to the right people to help me understand what I was experiencing.

When I awoke the next morning, I could see clearly around the house, but my head still felt foggy. Then I heard myself say, "I am going to seminary." The words shocked me, and I wondered where they came from. Was I not working with the sea turtles? Didn't it take me over a year to submit the application? Didn't I beat the odds by accomplishing what I had already managed to accomplish?

I had conflicting feelings: extreme joy at the prospect of seminary and immense loss for leaving the turtle program. That day, I applied for seminary, then immediately connected with several people who were familiar with seminary, to start enquiring about the process.

In the meantime, I questioned myself: "Can I do both? Or can I finish doing one more term with the turtles and then start seminary?" Five weeks later, I received word from both UCF and the seminary on the same day. Both were letters of acceptance. I cried hard for three days and endured a dichotomy of emotions over which path to take. I knew I could not truly give all of myself to either of them if I tried doing both at the same time.

My heart spoke while I was still uncertain. I figured the situation was a win either way. That afternoon, I called Doc and told him, "Like a woman in labor knows that her child is coming out, I know that I am going to seminary." I hoped he understood. I loved the sea turtles and the experiences I had with them. In the future, I added, I will accept any opportunity to work with them again. Then I sent my acceptance letter to the seminary.

Looking back now, I'm not certain that seminary was the right decision. Please don't misunderstand me, I believe the benefits from seminary were abundant, but I feel I have unfinished business in the biology world.

It is difficult when your life path diverges into two and you have to determine which is right. There is no guarantee you'll make the right choice. For me, I chose one path and now that I have completed that life scenario, I have the freedom to try another. There are endless possibilities, which could include addressing my unfinished business in the biology world.

Do you remember that little voice that filled my head with horrible thoughts after my Emmaus weekend? Well, it loved to antagonize me throughout my years at the seminary. After I started classes, my neurologist decided it would be good for me to receive the high-dose IV solumedrol (steroid) every eight weeks for a three-to-five-day dose, depending on my need. This was to help prevent school stress from exacerbating my symptoms.

The IV medication worked well. It served the purpose of getting me through seminary, although it came with its own set of issues. Every time I went on the steroids, I experienced a plethora of side effects and temporary exacerbation of symptoms: cloudy mind, dizziness, sinus issues, and thrush in the mouth, among others too personal to write here. At times, I found it difficult to focus well or complete assignments in a timely manner.

Whenever I took the IV steroids, the side effects interfered with my ability to drive safely. This meant I had to ask someone to take me to the infusion center to receive the medication. Then, if I had a class on that same day, someone also needed to drive me an hour each way to and from Orlando, and sit in class for several hours with me. I had to ask that person to commit an entire day to me alone. I felt as if I were an inconvenience and a burden to the people who had to drive me. In these moments, that little voice resurfaced and told me that I could not finish school and I was wasting money.

In times like this, I needed to remain strong in my faith that I made the right decision.

The unexpected love from people became my most powerful silver linings. The first one of this kind came during the second term at seminary and correlated with my first round of IV steroids. Shane Shepherd was one of the students I met at the middle school when my family moved to Lebanon, Indiana, in 1985. I had not talked to him since before I moved into my dad's house in 1988. Unexpectedly, out of nowhere, in 2011, he found me on Facebook and asked for my address. Within a week, he contacted me to say I should be expecting a package within a couple days. Wow! I had value. I already felt loved by my family and local friends, but this was over-the-top special because it was not expected. The gift was not elaborate, but it made me feel like a queen. It was a king cake from New Orleans, which is used in celebration of Mardi Gras.

People need to understand that sometimes the smallest gestures can bring forth a much greater response than the more elaborate ones. Shane and Sandra Shepherd from Lebanon, Indiana, had no idea how much inspiration and motivation they gave me to keep walking and to stay on the right path until my first book came out. Their gesture showed me that I was worth all the implied inconveniences the voice within my mind continued taunting. At the end of the term, as academics became more challenging, I ruminated on what my friends did for me, and that ignited my soul to reengage my efforts to complete the term.

Each term gradually became more difficult. Course work was more demanding. Responsibilities at home increased when we invited two teenaged boys to come live with us. Shortly afterwards, my neurologic issues became more serious. I started feeling fatigued, I lacked cognitive ability, and I constantly felt drained. If I was going to complete the goal of obtaining my graduate degree, I needed to stay strong and keep my focus only on the positives, I reminded myself constantly. The friends who became silver linings brought nothing but positives, like Sandra and Shane. They made it possible for me to attain this important personal goal.

Seminary taught me about myself. During my pre-seminary years, I had created a religious bubble, where I believed I was responsible for seeking people to convert. Seminary popped that bubble. Now I believe that God's intention is for us to go out and live the Bible. Of course, knowing scripture is important for personal accountability.

In my World Religions course, I learned that every religious affiliation has at least one part of God's plan for eternal life right, but no one has the whole picture entirely correct. I believe that in the end, all the different religious beliefs will meld together in some fashion.

My class visited several Buddhist communities and a Muslim mosque. It was a privilege to visit with other faith-based groups, to learn how they worship. Of my time at the seminary, I benefitted the most from this course. It was the one responsible for opening my eyes and popping my *holy* bubble.

Another course I gleaned much from was Cultural Studies, probably for very similar reasons shared with the World Religions course. Humanity differs in customs, habits, and ways of living, all around the globe. We might worship differently, but we have a connection through love.

Since completing my seminary studies, I have had no clear direction to follow—or since completing my studies in biology, for that matter. I imagine, then, that a concise occupational call is most likely a moot point for me, at least for right now.

The bottom line is that I don't have to know where I'm going right now. In fact, I know that yesterday's life call is not necessarily what my life's call is for today. I will just take one day at a time and do what I can to lift others in times of their own trials.

# Chapter 18
# The Unexpected Move

Early in 2010, NASA officially announced that the space shuttle program was closing and massive layoffs were immanent. When Chip's boss discussed the waves of layoffs looming over his department, we took that notice as a cue to search for other employment.

Chip received two job offers. One was local, but the pay was not enough to cover our current expenses. The second offer was on the other side of the state, in Tampa. The one in Tampa appeared much better because the pay was enough to cover expenses for a rental there and our mortgage in Titusville—or so we thought.

After packing and moving to Tampa, we realized the move and the job were both mistakes. We had not considered that the higher income would take us to a new income bracket, causing a significant reduction in take-home pay. Add that to a cost of living that amounted to twice what we were paying in Titusville before the move. We ended up more upside-down financially than if Chip had taken the Titusville job.

While we were trying to wrap our minds around the income situation at the new house in Tampa, something worse came along. A rat infestation and a malfunctioning air conditioning unit together created deplorable living conditions. For health reasons, at the recommendation of a doctor, we moved out of that house and into another one after living in the first only six weeks. The cost of moving twice in two months absorbed every last dime we had—and then some.

The second rental property was much more pleasant. We were renting from a physician who was super-nice. He let us paint walls and he frequently checked on us and quickly repaired issues that arose. This home was probably one of the most beautiful that I have ever lived in. So much so, that I incorporated some of its structural design into our house after we moved back to Titusville.

Good news in the middle of our chaos was that I received long-awaited news about my undergraduate college research. After two other journals turned me down, the Southeastern Association of Fish and Wildlife Agencies (SEAFWA) accepted my manuscript for publication.[8] A requirement for publishing was that I present my submission at an annual conference. I was thrilled that my persistence had finally paid off.

---

[8] Publication information is in Appendix A.

In October 2010, my dad and Phyllis flew into town to stay with the kids while Chip and I went off to Biloxi for the SEAFWA conference. Through persistence and faith, I was able to walk through extremely difficult life circumstances and keep a steady pace toward my goal of getting the research published.

Our move to Tampa had another positive side effect. It was the perfect opportunity for me to quit smoking. I had smoked off and on for over fifteen years. In 2008, I made the decision to quit. However, I was never able to stop smoking for much more than a couple of months. I started telling myself that if I could make it to a full year without smoking, I would claim a victory. I successfully quit smoking after we moved into the second house in Tampa.

My greatest struggle in the trip to Biloxi was related to my smoking challenge. The trip took place only two weeks after my quit date. The reason for my struggle was the conference location. I had to walk through a casino to reach the conference rooms.

Picture this: In the morning, I was gripping the nicotine patch on my arm super-tight, as if I were preventing it from falling off, while holding my breath and attempting to run through plumes of cigarette smoke. By afternoon, I walked slowly through the casino while attempting to suck in everyone's second-hand smoke. The next morning I was ready to yank off my patch and join the ranks of the smokers. I did not find this ordeal funny at all. However, when you ask Chip, he will tell you he was selling tickets to watch my silliness. I am happy to announce that I did not crack! In fact, I have more than seven years of smo-briety under my belt.

As we approached Christmas of 2010, I longed to go back to our neighborhood in Titusville. I missed our house and wished we had never moved. It probably did not help that I drove back there at least once every month just because I could. I started thinking that if we could go back to our house just for Christmas, maybe I would fulfill my desire to be there and it would be easier for me to return to Tampa. These thoughts ultimately lead to more than just visiting our house.

Looking back, I can see the necessity for moving away from our Titusville home. Two major changes occurred during that time that were imperative for my health. First, I quit smoking. The second one was regular exercise. I started my exercise program by walking regularly and then I joined a gym. Before long, I was feeling healthier than I had in years.

I can find a silver lining in homesickness.

# Chapter 19
# An Angel Called Robin

Our family had an annual tradition of sharing a family dinner with friends, then going as a group to the annual Christmas parade in downtown Titusville. In December 2010, we hoped to continue that tradition in our new city. However, since we moved to Tampa, we were no longer near our friends. I researched local activities in the new area. Unfortunately, I did not find a Christmas parade in close proximity. That is when I convinced Chip that our family should return to our Titusville house. We could not afford much during this Christmas season because of the costs of moving to Tampa and the additional cost to move out of the house of horrors where we first lived. However, we had enough money to get back to Titusville and stay there for the weekend.

Because our house had not yet sold, we still had utilities hooked up and we had furniture set up for staging to help it sell, so there was no need to stay at a hotel. We packed our fake Christmas tree, the kids, and the dogs and headed for home. Wayne and Carol had been friends and neighbors since we first moved to our new-construction home in Titusville in May 2006. Their grandson, Brett, was the same age as our son TJ, and when Brett lived with his grandparents, the two boys hung out together.

I was so excited to return for the weekend. The plan was for Carol to cook a fantastic meal, as she always did. Then Jackie and Robin would join my family as we headed to Wayne and Carol's house, where we would eat as a family and then head out for the Christmas parade in a group.

On the drive to our Titusville house, I tried unsuccessfully to contact Robin several times. Each time I called, I left her a message. Finally, I telephoned Jackie to see if she knew anything about Robin. She said she had not heard from her, either. We figured Robin was going through one of her "I want to be by myself" moods and we did not push the issue.

On the day of the parade, Jackie drove to my house and we went to Wayne and Carol's for dinner. Jackie and I talked about stopping by Robin's trailer to check on her, but we did not want to interrupt her if she was working through something. She was the kind of person who would contact us when she was ready. We respected that and went to the parade without her. The day after the parade, my family and I made the long drive back to our rental property in Tampa.

On the return trip, I attempted again to contact Robin. This was now becoming an uncharacteristically long quiet spell for her, especially when she had been so excited about my visit. I called Jackie and asked if she would stop by Robin's trailer. Because it was already very late at night, she told me she would go the next day, while she was running errands.

On Monday, Jackie went by Robin's trailer several times. One time she walked around the trailer and knocked at all the windows, yelling, "Robin!" She called me early that evening to ask if she should call the police. She explained that there was only one light on in the trailer; it was the bathroom light. Jackie checked the screen door. The door had been locked from the inside. That meant Robin was home. The litter box on the porch was very full, which was not characteristic of Robin. She was meticulous about cleaning it twice a day. Another sign of trouble was that her bedroom window was open. We'd just had several below-freezing days back-to-back with record low temperatures for us. Robin would not have left her windows open, especially not without plugging in a space heater. I told Jackie that she should call the police.

In the past, whenever Robin was having serious issues that required help, she called me on speed dial and I always jumped to help her. During a conversation I had with Robin less than a week prior to this day, she seemed more excited about seeing me than at any other time I can remember. She had recently completed several major improvements to her trailer, and she said she was anxious to share them with me. However, suddenly no one had seen her or heard from her in more than four days. All of the signs around her house indicated that something was very wrong—much more than usual. I had a feeling of dread come into my gut, much like when I learned of Ruth's death. I now feared that Robin was dead.

Even though Jackie did not smell the "smell of death" near the open window, she too felt that those signs meant Robin was either seriously injured or she had died. "Gretchen, it may be a long night," she warned me when we spoke again. I asked her to call me when the police arrived. If Robin was dead, I planned to make the two-hour drive back immediately.

Chip insisted that I should try to eat, just in case. He prepared food for me, and as I was eating, Jackie called. The police had arrived and they asked her to stay back because they needed to break in. "We don't know what we'll find," they warned her. Chip and I were silent as we sat awaiting confirmation of our fears. One of the officers returned outside after only a minute. He was shaking his head. Robin was in the trailer. She was dead.

I probably shouldn't have left for the long drive then because I was very upset. However, with Robin's family living so far away, Chip, the kids, and I had become her family. "How could I not have been there for her?" I asked myself. I knew I needed to be with her now.

Fortunately, I hadn't unpacked after our weekend away. I left my full plate of food on the table, grabbed my bag, added a couple of things, and headed out. Two hours later, I sat outside Robin's trailer, mourning this loss. It had been ten days since we last spoke, and I already missed her. Upon reflection, I celebrated her tremendous personal growth in life, compared to when we first met. I was confident in saying she had a most amazing welcome home when she arrived at the pearly gates of Heaven.

Robin was an only child whose dad was suffering from Alzheimer's and her mom from multiple strokes. Considering their health and the wintry weather at their home in Maryland, compounded with the news about their daughter's death, meant they could not travel or handle these end-of-life issues. Having just done this for Ruth, I was in an optimum position to assume the role. Additionally, because we had adopted Robin as part of our family, I naturally assumed the familial role with her parents. I did everything I could to help.

In spite of the cold, I offered to stay as long as I needed to. It was wonderful how specific people were able to help based on the needs of the moment. One example is that Robin passed away in her bed, and her body lay there for four days, the police estimated. One friend came on the first day to help move the mattress to the porch. She came back once more, later in the week, to help me go through the outside storage.

Another example happened when Lowell Gray helped Wanda and me haul the mattress to the dump. He was perfect for that job because he was blessed with an inability to smell. Even though it was cold, the overwhelming stench of death was rancid. Every time Wanda and I felt like vomiting from the smell, he was there to help us.

Wanda was the one person who stayed with me every day throughout the entire event. We developed a new kind of sisterly love, as we both experienced something so deep and final together. The most emotional days for me were the ones where Jackie, Wanda, and I worked together cleaning Robin's trailer. It brought back tender memories of the Emmaus weekend we had shared with Robin.

Every day I kept regular contact with Robin's mom about what we were to do with various items. We separated the trash, items to donate, and important keepsakes. I did the best I could to get the most important items to her mom as quickly as possible. It was almost

Christmas and it was not fair that anyone should have to deal with end-of-life details for a loved one during the Christmas season. I wanted to wade through the job as quickly as possible, so I felt I couldn't stop working long enough to sleep. By Friday, I scheduled an appointment with my former doctor after becoming very sick during the cleanup process. Chip was worried and decided I should not drive home that weekend. Instead, he packed the kids and puppies and drove to our house.

At some point during the cleanup at Robin's, I found an envelope addressed to me. I cannot describe the feelings that swamped me as I read the letter, because I truly felt this message came straight from Robin herself. The actual writer was my beautiful friend Jackie, but it was as if Robin had given her the perfect words to write. For a moment, I felt as if I was face to face with Robin and she was telling me how much I meant to her and how much she appreciated the help I was offering in her end of life affairs.

The letter read:

*Hi, sweet Gretchen!*

> *I know that gas prices and tolls really bite, and still you came all the way over here because you love me and wanted to do whatever you could to help. Dear Gretchen, please fill up the truck with my compliments; it is the least I can do for someone who loves me as you do! You are the sister I never had; well, I guess you could have been my daughter from when I was really young, but the point is, you have loved me in life, and you love me enough to*

*help my parents here in my death. I hope you can feel my love for you! ...*

*Gretchen, please don't cry long for me. Smile when you remember the great times we had together, and the laughter, and the silly things I did. Please, just think of me when you see a beautiful horse galloping through a green field, and when you see sailboats cruising gently along. Think of me when you hear Jimmy Buffet singing "Margaritaville," and the laughter we shared. I will always treasure our time together. You really helped me to change my life!*

*Always feel my love, Gretchen!*

*Signed,*

*Your Robin*

Jackie was the friend who not only wrote this beautiful letter, but also included the cash to fill my truck with gas. She truly was a silver lining for me on this stage of my life walk.

In mid-January 2011, Ashley and I drove back to our house in Titusville to close on the sale of Robin's trailer. Fortunately, the sale fell through, which made it available for an old trailer park friend of Robin's, who was in a desperate situation. She did not have much money and her trailer became uninhabitable just as we were expecting more freezing weather. It felt right to sell her the trailer at a lower price than I was originally asking. We closed the deal that very day, for a price she could afford.

While Ashley and I were in Titusville for the sale, I took that opportunity to put together a small celebration of life for Robin. About eight people came together for this gathering. Two of the women were friends of Robin's from the days when she lived in the marina, and they attended our church. The others who joined me were my daughter Ashley, Jackie, and Wanda, as well as Lowell and his beautiful wife Jean, who hosted the event at their house. It was wonderful to hear the various stories and see how Robin's life came full-circle from her life's trials to finding her peace.

I believe the fruit of patience that developed within me during my medical trials was ripe at this time. Through patience, I could exude a depth of love, forgiveness, and guidance for this fantastic woman. I do not take credit for her personal transformation, but I believe I placed a few drops into her bucket of faith. Likewise, I feel that she, too, added a few drops into my bucket, which became part of a silver lining for me.

# Chapter 20
# Back on Track and the New Boys

In January 2011, after the trailer situation was resolved, Ashley and I felt like sticking around our house in Titusville for a bit longer. When it crossed my mind that she had another day off from school, making it possible for us to stay yet another day, we felt the excitement of building ideas. I called Chip and said, "Here's the scoop: Ashley and I have been talkin' and we've decided we're not coming back." Stunned but not surprised, he asked, "Do you mean forever, or that you're not coming back on Sunday?"

I told him we were *never* coming back.

"Negative," he said. "You will come back to get the boy child first. HA!"

Ashley and I stayed the extra day and then returned to the rental house in Tampa, where Chip and I resumed the conversation about moving back to our house in Titusville. We knew he would have to search for a new job before he could leave Tampa and afford the move back to Titusville. This was a decision for which we were all willing to make sacrifices in order to accomplish. The kids and I returned to our house in Titusville and Chip made himself a geo-bachelor, where he lived with a friend in Tampa during the week and with us in Titusville on the weekends.

Our decision to move back to Titusville as soon as possible was an attempt to return the kids to normalcy as soon as possible. Funny, but even though we did not buy anything new during our transition, we seemed to have much more stuff on our return. We could not fit it all into the moving truck. Our resolution was to pack the Chevy Avalanche – vertical – and tie everything down with ropes.

When we arrived back in town, Jackie was waiting in our driveway. She said we looked like *"The Beverly Hillbillies return home."* The next morning, I took the house off the market and Chip began networking for a job closer to our home. Until he landed a job, we only saw him on the weekends. With his vigorous efforts, he received an offer of a computer science job back at Kennedy Space Center, so he rejoined us after only two months.

Our return to Titusville lined up perfectly with the start of my classes in February 2011. This was my original planned timing for attending seminary. Starting seminary was my first legitimate attempt at setting life goals for myself that were just outside of my comfort zone and perceived capability. Seminary classes forced me to utilize all of my energy in attending and completing them.

My first term back at college, coupled with the need to reorient our family back to life together after our reunion in Titusville, became a huge strain on my neurologic health. I started having issues with balance, fine motor skills, and overall functioning abilities. My health was bad enough to require IV steroids to calm my neurologic issues. This was the first time I had to go on the steroids in almost four years, and that upset me. I started asking myself if going to college was causing me irreversible damage.

This is when Sandra and Shane Shepherd crossed my path with a king cake.

Their gesture helped me realize that I had value to someone in a time when I significantly doubted myself. Second, the cake was so full of color that it represented hope and a bright future. I felt warmth, blessing, love, and cheer from that one simple gift. There are just no words to articulate the significance of this simple gesture. It meant the world to me, especially after enduring the difficult walk I had been on for the previous several years. I received this cake as an act of love, which set me in the right mind for completing my first term at seminary. I call Shane and Sandra silver linings in my life.

Before we relocated to the rental property in Tampa, Chip and I felt a heavy tug on our hearts to adopt a girl of middle school age. The move caused us to question this decision. When we returned to our house in Titusville, we felt it was time to pursue this venture, so we signed up for adoption classes. At the conclusion, we realized that maybe we weren't intended to legally adopt a child since we were having no luck finding a good match in the adoption community. However, because we had two kids, there were always teenagers in and out of our house. The classes prepared us to bring teens under our wings and love them into the right direction—and that is just what we did.

We added two boys to our family through love, not the judicial system, because they were over the legal age of eighteen. The first young man was Brett Ricks, Wayne and Carol's grandson. The second young man was Ryan Wensel. Both of my kids and Brett knew Ryan from the Junior ROTC at the high school. My kids were excited to have them join our family because, TJ and Ashley informed me, they had always wanted more siblings. It also meant that they could share chores with more help available.

I believe these two young men found something in our family that they needed. One became a full-time resident, and the other became a part-time resident in our house after we invited them in at the end of January 2013.

Brett's reputation was that of a bully—but, like a Chihuahua, he was all bark and no bite. He ran his mouth, but when it came time to follow through with the actions to support his words, there were no actions. To us, he always seemed to be trying to protect himself from deeper hurts. He yearned to be the center of attention as a sign of acceptance, and he didn't feel like he received attention from many people. Unfortunately for Brett, once he found himself in a situation where things were going very well, he always managed to sabotage his success. He would find himself hurting and having to start over.

Brett was living with his grandparents as he headed into his last term of high school in the spring of 2013. By this point, he had created a reputation for himself with teachers, students, and the administration that threatened to keep him from graduating. This was a culmination of not turning in assignments, being disrespectful to teachers and administrators, and running his mouth with students. His grandparents could handle doing all that was necessary to get him to graduation, but their jobs' peak season was in the spring, which directly corresponded with Brett's last term in high school.

Chip and I offered to take him in for that last term to help him tackle this major hurdle. We spent hours of one-on-one time with Brett to help him with his academics. We also made multiple trips to the high school to meet with teachers and administrators, resolving all kinds of school-related issues, from missing assignments to his attitudes while dealing with others. By the end of the term, Brett was completing all of his assignments. He even put his behavior in check, at least as well as he could. Ultimately, he did what he needed to do, and he successfully completed high school.

Brett does not come around very often anymore, but we always enjoy hearing about how he's doing and what his next life adventures are.

When we brought Ryan into our house at the end of January 2013, he was looking for direction. He moved in during the same term we were helping Brett. This was the last term in school for the boys, as well as me. Ryan quickly showed us he was extremely self-sufficient and capable of motivating himself. His main need was to have time to be a kid without heavy pressures, and he needed to learn how to focus. We realized he needed to learn how to burn off some youthful energy and desires in order to start concentrating on his future. After moving into our house, he picked up two part-time jobs and bought a vehicle. After graduation, he went to a recruiter and joined the service.

During the spring of 2013, my house was hopping busy. Of the six people under my roof, we never knew who was coming, going, turning around, or upside down. I LOVED it. When things got bad, they did not fester long enough to feel the full impact before the situation turned amazing. We took the time to celebrate everything.

On the very same day that May, the boys and I dressed in caps and gowns for our graduations. My commencement was in the morning, theirs was that evening, and the next day we had a full-blown luau bash to celebrate our accomplishments. Eleven days later, I celebrated my fortieth birthday. As the dust settled from these extreme events with such emotional highs, Cristi contacted me and offered to come for a visit. I then began planning a visitor in my house for the next month.

While Chip and I faced great difficulties during this stage of our lives, I believe there were equal amounts of personal growth and celebrations of major accomplishments. Because we could not take this pivotal yet chaotic life walk with our own strength, we leaned heavily on our faith. We gained many tools and silver linings during this time. I won't say they made the walk easy, but they certainly made it possible.

# Chapter 21
# A Living Angel Named Jennilee

The military had moved me all over the country after I was married the first time in 1994. Once I married Chip in 1997, the military moved us several more times. Then, in 2001, when Chip switched from active duty to reserve status with the military, we moved again in search of the right climate to help me with my disease. It was finally time to settle down in May 2006, when we moved into our newly constructed house. We had no intentions of moving out of our house before both TJ and Ashley graduated from high school.

The darkest days with my MS occurred shortly after we settled into our house in 2006. Because the kids were only starting to develop friendships, their new friends did not see repercussions from these darkest MS trials. This spared them from witnessing how scary-bad the disease really was. However, as time rolled forward, several of their friends saw micro-glimpses of my symptoms. Either they came to visit when I was in the middle of an exacerbation and they saw my inability to do things properly or they saw me with the IV during treatment. On those occasions, though, they could see that I was managing the disease quite well. Our lives were not so scary.

In the four years between moving into our new home in Titusville and our move to Tampa, our kids had developed strong bonds with their friends. We had fully anticipated that they would develop their best relationships ever in Titusville. While TJ was very introverted and had only a few friends, they were among his best friends ever. These boys did not participate in school functions; they spent most of their time as homebodies, playing video games. Ashley, on the other hand, was quite active with school and her friends. Chip and I dearly loved all of her friends and their parents. It was as if we all became part of the same family. In fact, when the girls had school functions and award ceremonies, all the parents sat together to cheer them on. The parents became the girls' biggest cheerleaders—that was a textbook example of a village raising the children.

It was difficult for my family to make the move to Tampa. We were all so tired of moving and had finally lived in a house longer than three years. What would happen to the relationships we had created? Would they remain after we moved? We looked for ways to reduce the hardship of a move—especially for Ashley, because she was in middle school, the worst time to move with a teenaged girl.

In an attempt to help Ashley adjust to the move, we brought a couple of her friends with us to Tampa the day we went to sign our rental agreement. This way, the girls could see the house we were moving into and help leave behind some happy memories for Ashley. Unfortunately, this day strained my health dramatically, causing the girls to experience the ugly side of my disease.

We arrived at the Tampa house in July 2010 for our walk-through. Even though this was the hottest time of the year, the realty company had failed to turn the air conditioning on. I figured I would be okay if we didn't stay there too long. An hour later, we were finally done with the walk-through and headed over to the management office to sign the documents. That office also did not have the air conditioning turned on, and the building was very hot. We explained to the realtor that I had MS and the heat was very bad for me. We asked the realtor if he could cool the place down. He said no, that he would make the visit quick. For the record, it was not quick; I have never signed so many documents for a rental property before.

My vision became blurry. I found it was difficult to hold the pen. I told Chip that I was scared. I felt trapped, as if something bad was about to happen and I could do nothing to stop it. I got up from the table and walked into the hallway looking for cooler air. Just as I stepped out of the room, I collapsed onto the floor. Chip rushed over and scooped my unresponsive body off the floor. He ran with me to the truck, where he blasted cold air conditioning on me. He also bought a ten-pound bag of ice and wrapped my arms around it, to cool my core body temperature.

In the midst of this crisis situation, with Chip ready to take me to the Emergency Room, we had two of Ashley's friends with us. Thoughts of how scared the girls must be as they watched this happen raced through my head, but I could do nothing to change the situation. I remember praying that we wouldn't have to go to the hospital. I just wanted to get home. Fortunately, Chip's quick thinking and the cooling measures helped me in time. We decided that I did not need to go to the hospital, so we could return the girls safely to their homes in Titusville.

That was just one example of our children's friends watching the scary neurologic beast. So, what happens when one of them experiences her own scary neurologic beast?

The girls were in the second term of sophomore year in high school during the spring of 2012, when Jennilee started having issues alarmingly similar to my own. Jennilee is a bubbly, high-spirited young lady packed into a super-small body. She has high aspirations of becoming the next great Steven Spielberg. Imagine the fears she had about her future when she woke up one morning with odd skin sensations that covered her body and an inability to use her right hand. In her stubbornness, she decided to go to school and work through it. After doing this for a week, her mom decided Jennilee needed medical attention. The doctor said everything looked fine and sent her home. "You just need more sleep," he advised.

When her mom explained her symptoms to me, I remember thinking they sounded a great deal like my own neurologic symptoms. My gut rolled at the idea that one of my daughter's friends could also have MS. I told Jennilee's mother that while they sounded like my symptoms, there could be so many other causes. "Just give it some time," I suggested.

Jennilee continued having issues with her hand, preventing her from taking the abundant notes she needed. The frustrations convinced her mom to take her back to the doctor. This time he started running tests on her. The MRI revealed one lesion in her brain. Yes, she had only one lesion and one neurologic episode. However, to have a diagnosis of multiple sclerosis, the scan must reveal multiple lesions. Additionally, an MS diagnosis requires two separate neurologic episodes affecting two different areas of the body, each separated by time. This was not the case with Jennilee, so the doctor sent her home, promising, "We will continue to watch this." After three weeks, the symptoms went away.

During the summer 2013, Jennilee and her family spent an entire week at the beach in the sun. By the end of the week, Jennilee was not feeling well. She had intense pain in her skin. When it was touched, it felt as if her skin was seared. Clothing, hair, necklaces, wind, anything that touched her skin, evoked that same response. By the end of the day, a new and extremely uncomfortable symptom appeared. She felt the sensation of needles in her feet. By morning, this sensation covered her body from her feet to her shoulders. Her stomach felt as if it was sticking a mile out, bloated, and Jennilee's mind felt disoriented. She went to her parents in tears, concerned and scared.

"She needs to be admitted. Bring her in now, so we can run more tests," doctors ordered, when Jennilee's parents called them. The MRI revealed two more lesions in her brain. Now they could diagnose her with MS and start her on intravenous steroids to reduce the inflammation in her brain. The timing of her admittance to the hospital corresponded with the IV infusion that I was receiving after I completed graduate school in the summer of 2013.

Jennilee was hospitalized for a full week and given IV steroids before her symptoms started to wane. They completely subsided after she returned home and was weaned off the steroids. During her week in the hospital, she and I spent time chatting with each other through Facebook and texts. In this way, I did what I could to lift her spirits. I hoped she could see that we were a team fighting the same battle together.

Jennilee is a very strong young lady, and she is going to keep living in spite of this diagnosis. She continues to go to school and does all she can to stay as active and "normal" as she possibly can. Sometimes people want to do things for her, others want to make things easier for her, and yet she just wants life to remain the same as it was before the diagnosis. I believe she can have a similar life as long as she continues doing what she can while she can.

Since her diagnosis, Jennilee reminded me about how inspiring my life with MS has been for her new walk. "I remember looking up to you, because even though it was clear to see that MS could be very challenging and so demolishing to both your will and your spirit, Miss Gretchen, there you were, still smiling and facing life," she said. "I loved seeing that. Even in your worst times, I saw how you turned the negative situation around. Now I believe that no matter what I face, even if it is not the same magnitude, I can handle it. If you can do it, if you can turn a horrid situation around, then I certainly can, too."

She added, "I remember you telling me if I was diagnosed with MS, I was going to be okay. When the diagnosis came, and I learned I was stricken with the very same disease you deal with, you became the angel on my doorstep." She added with a heartfelt note that I totally understood, "I will be honest, I was very frightened, not knowing what having MS was going to mean for me, but watching you helped me so much. I looked at you with a new understanding. I learned that having an episode of MS can be so terrible, just utterly debilitating in every way. However, even when you were having an episode, you were still doing everything you wanted... sure, some days you struggled but you didn't let MS stop you from enjoying the things you love in life. It was from that moment that I stopped fearing my disease. I knew if you could handle it, then so could I. Miss Gretchen, you were the perfect example of that."

Jennilee spoke about the peace I gave her mom, who, I knew, was so upset that she felt that her world would not quit spinning. They both saw me as someone who understood and could help them walk through this new life walk. Jennilee said, "Miss Gretchen, you helped me to get the acceptance I have today. I do not fear my disease, the possibilities of going blind or losing my abilities to walk. I don't fear the medication I give myself every week. I don't fear tomorrow, because I know that no matter how hard it gets, no matter what MS throws at me, I have my faith to get me through every single step of the way. Then, when it is too much for my flesh and bone to handle, when the tears are streaming down my cheeks because I cannot dress myself or apply my own makeup, I stop, take a deep breath, and remind myself that God is standing with me and strengthening me. It was you, Miss Gretchen, from the beginning, who helped me get this attitude and acceptance. So, thank you!"

This young lady thinks I'm very strong. She makes me feel like a super hero! I am so thankful our paths crossed. While I'm almost halfway through my life walk, she is just beginning hers. I cannot put words to the effect I have had on her life, but I am so grateful I was able to be that light, a silver lining for her.

I am hopeful that the inspiration she found in me is enough to keep her forward momentum. Jennilee is immensely intelligent, and she has great plans for going to college and becoming a movie director. This walk for her includes a rather large burden to bear. Many of her peers will not understand, yet I believe she will persevere to attain all her goals. She will be a shining star, all on her own, for so many others she has yet to meet.

The same week, in June 2013, when Jennilee and I were both receiving intravenous steroids for our MS episodes, we both had friends walking with us—literally and figuratively. This was when Cristi came to my house for a long-overdue visit. She drove me to the infusion center. Friends are some of the best silver linings.

# Chapter 22
# Re-connecting with Cristi

Out of the ashes of my past, in 2013, I reconnected with Cristi, after ten years of separation. Even during those years apart, I thought of her often. Every time I was overcome by desperation and looking for my faith, I was thankful Cristi had helped me invite God into my heart that night in her room. All those years ago, when I was sixteen, I was drawn to her house for a reason. Now she was being drawn to my house.

When we got on the phone with each other, Cristi said that she truly believed that she needed to come to my house for an extended stay. My heart could tell that Cristi was going through her own storms. Even before she talked about coming to my house, I knew that something was guiding her to me and that I was supposed to stay clear of the reasons. No anticipations.

At the time, I was actively involved in three very different churches and with the Order of St. Luke healing ministry at two other churches. My plan was to let Cristi come to my house and gain exposure to everything I was doing. Maybe something I was undergoing would become a silver lining to help her out of her current storm.

She arrived at my house a month after the three graduations (two high school and my graduate school), just in time for my next round of IV steroids. The timing was awesome. Chip let Cristi take me to the infusion center and hang out for the long hours of infusion. We were able to catch up on lost time, how our lives had squirrelled around very different challenges and issues. Best of all, she shared her experiences traveling in Israel. As she sat next to me sharing the pictures, I felt like I was physically experiencing her visit to Jerusalem along with her.

At the infusion center, Cristi experienced some of the same joys I do at that place—yes, I am being facetious. The bottom line is that I have choices: I can go to that place and cry my eyes out because it sucks as badly as it does, or I could intentionally seek humor. Humor is my favorite thing to find.

When I am on the IV steroids, especially at the beginning, there is entirely too much humor to experience. The ladies who work there are awesome and they seemed to enjoy the humor that follows me into that building. What was it they once told me? Oh, yes: "You never know what you are going to get when Gretchen comes through the door."

I have gone to the IV infusion center enough times to develop a pattern. It goes like this... When I walk through the door, I see Ollie at the front desk. She is a no-nonsense woman who is full of spirit. I always stop by to let her know I am there, say good morning, and tell her how beautiful she is. Then Ollie tells me what room number is mine. I take my purse, jacket, and drink to the room and set them on my chair. On the way to the bathroom, I say hello to my two regular nurses, Jeannine and Sylvia. By the time I return to my chair, either Ollie or the nurses have guided whoever is with me, usually Chip, to my room.

After I return to my chair, I sign admission papers and have vital signs taken. My nurse gets the IV in place, and we start treatment. This time, June 2013, Cristi was my support person.

Okay, so on day one of the steroids, my room was directly across the hall from the bathroom. Cristi had been sharing pictures with me of her trip to Israel. I had to go to the bathroom, but I was so excited about her pictures that I just held it. That was a big mistake, because once I realized I could not wait any longer, I was afraid I would not make it across the hall before my bladder popped. Cristi decided to stay in my room while I took my IV pole on a walkabout to the bathroom. This maneuver was skewed, since my lower body stayed to the left, along with my butt, while I intentionally pushed my upper body in the opposite direction, towards the rest room.

My plan was to correct the misdirected lower part of my body. By this point, I was making a lot of noise because I could not coordinate my IV pole with my body's actions. The pole and my upper body went in one direction, while my lower body went the opposite. The noise I was making while trying to control my body's split mentality attracted an audience. Sylvia, one of my two fabulous nurses, managed to both catch and then push my tail end in the correct direction before I smashed into a wall. My body became correctly oriented just as I reached the bathroom door, when I felt my shoulder slightly clip the edge of the doorframe. But, victory! I was in the bathroom. Wahoo!

When the time came to return to my room, I stood in the open door of the bathroom and contemplated the situation. "It's only about six or seven good-sized steps between the bathroom door and my chair," I reminded myself. "If I just hold my breath and go real fast, I should be able to get from here to there without the same issues I had on the way to the bathroom." Okay, one … two … three … I held my breath and went for it. STEP-step.step.step.step … THUD … Ka-BLAMB! With that speed, I had excellent momentum to throw myself against the wall while completely missing the threshold of my door.

The problem was that my legs were still off, which oriented my stride to the left, causing me to miss the door completely. Instead, that whole physics momentum theory kicked in. My short quick steps rapidly propelled me forward until my IV pole hit the wall and I kept going until I smashed into both the IV pole and the wall.

Jeannine, my other fantastic nurse, and Cristi had the comical view as they saw me standing in the bathroom door. They watched me prepare to come across. Then, in the blink of an eye, I was not there… followed by the crash. This led them to begin a mad dash to my aid, where they found me dazed from the impact. I only momentarily felt defeated, realizing that my execution had failed so miserably. No matter, there were not many dry eyes, thanks to the laughter—including my own.

It sure feels good to find humor in situations that have the potential to be so dark. In this case, I had the added benefit of sharing this experience with Cristi. Nowadays when I have to return to the infusion center, as I have already done several times since she was there with me, I have fond memories to reflect upon. I did not have an awkward moment with Cristi at the infusion center; it just felt like the right thing to happen and the perfect time.

During Cristi's two-week stay, she experienced the crazy chaos of my house as we all tried to juggle my schedule with Chip's and the schedules of all those young adult people we had onboard with us. I did everything I could not to interject thoughts about what we were doing and where we were going. I made every effort to make sure Cristi was able to experience my life in all its craziness.

One night, my newest friend, Tammy, invited us to her church. She said there was a special healing event taking place. I thought it might be interesting to check it out. Tammy and I both decided that the event would probably benefit Cristi more than us, because Cristi was working through a major life storm. "For the sake of making sure you experience everything, maybe we should go," I told Cristi. She agreed.

At the church, I was standing between Cristi and Tammy, one of my oldest and one of my newest friends. We were sing-sing-singing songs when my legs started to feel like spaghetti under me. An unseen influence was powerfully strong in that place. I thought to myself, "Girl, you are NOT going down!" Then one of the church leaders, Rita, walked up to me, took my hand, and walked me to the front of the room, where people were actively praying with each other.

Rita leaned over me and spoke intimate details about my past, specifically relating to my mother and my need to forgive her. Yet she could not have known those things from any previous conversation with me; she did not know me from Adam. I went back to my seat and cried hard. When I calmed down, I stood up and began singing again.

Finally, our guest speaker was introduced. Although I knew he was there to do a healing service, I was a little skeptical. Still, I told myself, if anyone could be healed from the service, then great. He asked, "Is there anyone here suffering from a disease, who wants healing?" Of course, I raised my hand. I had been asking for freedom from this disease for years.

Sitting next to me, Cristi was so excited that she was aggressively pointing both of her index fingers at me. In a room packed solid with people, I just knew the speaker was going to address *me* first. And, sure enough, there he was, walking towards me from the opposite side of this huge room. He stopped right next to me and asked my name. Then he inquired about the disease.

As he took me by the hand and walked me to the front of the room, I thought, "Uh-oh, here we go again." I warned myself, "Girl, listen to me. We are staying off the floor—remember that."

When we reached the front of the room, he took my other hand and began to pray aloud. As he prayed, my legs again turned into spaghetti. However, I was NOT going to hit the floor at this church that was not my own! It took every effort I had to prevent myself from dropping to the floor like a heavy anvil. When he finished praying, I could not find any words on my tongue to speak. However, I immediately recognized that I had clearer vision. On the return to my seat, I stared around the room in amazement. I saw things I had not been able to see minutes before.

The focus of the event was on healing; you were either praying for healing or you were receiving prayer for healing. I had already received my prayer for healing. Now I wanted to focus on anyone but me.

While I was standing with my arms in the air, my legs began to give out. The seats in the room are like those in a movie theater; they spring closed when no one is sitting on them. I thought, if I stick my rear end out far enough and just drop, then I can catch myself on the edge of the seat and prevent my butt from hitting the floor. I successfully executed the plan.

Now that I was on the edge of the chair, I felt heavy, as if the floor was still calling my name. I thought to myself, "Okay, maybe if I drape my upper body over the seat in front of me, it will lock me in place, preventing further descent to the floor." As soon as I parked my head in the crook of my arm, a complete stranger approached me.

She leaned over me and said, "I am not a member of this church, but God told me to stop by and tell you…"

I can't remember exactly what she said, but I know that it deeply touched my heart.

What in the world? My number was up that night for sure. I had agreed to attend this function believing it was for Cristi. Now I was starting to wonder. Most of my thoughts that night had focused on keeping my butt off the floor – that same floor that refused to stop calling me.

Something about that stranger bringing a message from God made me realize I could no longer contain my emotions. The level of love and healing in that place was so powerful and palpable that no words can accurately articulate what was happening. I cried so hard I could barely breathe. I had so many tears that the mucous literally hung from my nose to the floor. Under normal circumstances, I might have been embarrassed. However, any energy I had left was dedicated to keeping my dang butt off the floor.

Unbeknownst to me, Tammy and Cristi had been watching my progression and they chuckled at my predicament. Together they came to an agreement that I should just go to the floor. Cristi said, "Wouldn't that just be easier?" Then Tammy added, "You should just let yourself go."

Something about those words sounded good. I was now sitting in the seat next to the aisle, so I eased myself out and just slightly to the side, where only my butt was on the floor and I was hanging onto the arm. Then Tammy firmly said, "Just let go." The moment I lifted my head and let go of the arm of the seat, BAM. I hit the floor. HARD. It was as if someone had aggressively shoved me to the ground.

I landed in a distorted pretzel-like position that I could not untangle on my own. I lay there, considering how odd the position felt—and must have looked. While I could neither move nor speak, the room began to feel like it would not stop moving. I spoke to God silently, in my head, and said, "I know you are doing something in me. This feels weird and I don't like it, but I trust that you are doing something good in me, so thank you. I love you so much! Thank you." I just kept thanking Him.

After long moments passed, I opened my eyes to see a stranger standing over me. I think it was Rita, but I cannot remember. I checked, and nope, I still could not talk or move. Therefore, I shut my eyes again.

After more time passed, Tammy and Cristi thought they needed to call Chip to come get us because I was the one who had driven there. Fortunately, however, I started moving on my own again.

I did not fully understand what happened that night, but I claimed it as something good for my restoration.

When the time came for Cristi to return home, she was much more affectionate than the day she arrived. On the day I picked her up at the airport, she seemed standoffish about giving me a hug. By the time she went home, she was hugging and saying, "I love you" to everyone. She said she truly felt blessed to have visited. "I'm not ready to go back home," she said. But she knew she had to.

The good news was that she went home a changed woman. What I knew before Cristi came was that she had something personal going on in her life that she needed to work out, and she felt convinced that my house was the place where she could do that. In this way, she could separate herself from her daily activities and contacts and open her eyes to Him at the various churches where I worshiped.

On that visit in 2013, Cristi experienced four different types of church services: a non-denominational service Chip and I were helping to launch, Tammy's non-denominational church, my Methodist church, and my Episcopalian church. The Order of St. Luke Healing Ministry took place at both the Episcopal and Methodist churches. Add to that the crazy chaotic life in my house with different schedules for six people. She found plenty to occupy her thoughts and time.

After arriving back home in Indiana, Cristi called and told me she regularly reflected on her time spent with me at my house. She mostly remembered how many people were there and how we were able to keep everyone's schedule straight, she said, laughing. To this day, she tells me that one of the first things she recognized was how much I served as a matriarch in the house, that everyone scheduled their activities around my abilities and schedule. "You're the one who leads household prayer regularly," she observed.

In our home, we eat dinners at the table, and that is where our regular communications take place, Cristi noticed. Away from our house, she gleaned a great deal from my various religious affiliations, specifically the Order of St. Luke Healing Ministry and the Episcopal Church. She allowed these experiences and connections to help her create a new life for herself when she returned home to Indiana.

The visit was not solely for Cristi's sake, however. We both benefited. Something about her visit gave me a sensation of completeness. I don't understand why, I just recognized the feeling. Neither Cristi nor I could have accomplished our regeneration on our own, but through a sincere desire and effort to connect by way of a deeply spiritual element, something happened for our mutual and greater good. I believe there is no substitute for power that comes when we utilize our entire spiritual body, especially with respect to trials. I am so thankful I said yes to Cristi's visit during that time. I feel more complete through this experience.

Cristi first became a significant silver lining after I was liberated from my mother's house of horrors, and she continues to enrich my life many years later. Meanwhile, however, while we reconnected and resumed our relationship, I was more recently forced to say goodbye to another significant silver lining, a rescuer from my disease. Her name is Zoey.

Zoey stayed right by my side me every day through the darkest days of my life. She rescued me from that devastating loneliness. She deserves a hero story of her very own, but for the sake of this book, you will meet her in the next chapter.

Phoebe Walker

# Chapter 23
# My heart, my Zoey

I live with a nightmare called multiple sclerosis and yet I continue to thrive in spite of this heinous disease. Truth be told, I do not believe I could survive what I did if it were not for daily contact with my live-in angel. Zoey. It was as if she had magical powers that allowed her to penetrate the cast iron capsule that multiple sclerosis inflicted on me, isolating me from life and plunging me into the deepest, darkest depths of terror and loneliness.

Have you ever had a pet that made you feel like you were the only thing in the world that mattered? That was my Zoey. While I've had several animals throughout the years, none can touch the deeply spiritual connection that Zoe and I shared. About eight weeks prior to writing this tribute, I had to say goodbye for now. As part of my healing from this enormous loss, I reflected on her great gifts and the role she played in my life.

Upon looking back, I believe she was sent directly to me for exactly this purpose, to help me survive the worst that MS would throw at me. In my survivor's guilt, I acknowledge that was a profound weight for such a small creature to shoulder. Her soul was made of steel and could handle the massive loads that she carried for me.

Come, let's go on a walk down memory lane to see this angel's purpose in my life.

The story begins with a young and feisty Yorkie puppy named Beans. He was the first dog we gave our kids; they were in elementary school at the time. Beans was given his name because he was very spastic, full of all kinds of extra energy, so I felt he needed a friend to keep him occupied.

Chip happened to be away on military orders when I concocted a crazy plan to get Beans a friend. For the record, I always made changes to the house when Chip was away. That was one of the many ways I coped with our time apart. So, while Chip was serving in June 2004, I set out on a quest to find a friend for Beans.

We were living in Campbellsville, Kentucky at this time. I didn't know much about the area or where to find puppies for sale, so I bought a newspaper and looked in the classified ads section. There, I found a Shih Tzu breeder near Elizabethtown and decided to make the drive.

When the kids and I walked through the door of the breeder's facility, I saw a very clean place where the animals were well cared for. Both the facility and the people who worked there made me feel confident that it was a good place to find a new puppy.

In the small room where they kept the puppies, there were nine cages, three in a row, with three rows stacked on each other. The cage right in the middle had the most adorable puppy I have ever seen. She became my Zoey. She had a super-cute little round face that resembled an Ewok from *Star Wars* and she had eyeballs so large that they seemed to fill her little face. Those eyes were staring right through me, to the deepest part of my heart—and there she imbedded an invisible hook with just one look. That was enough.

I had to hold her. Once I took her out of the cage, she immediately smothered my face in Zoey kisses and cuddled under my chin. "Okay, okay," I chuckled. "You are a cute one. Let's see what Beans says, because the reason I came here is to find him a friend."

A couple months prior, I had chosen Beans to keep the kids and me company during Chip's absences. This time around, while we were looking for a new puppy, I believe Zoey chose me. Once I put her on the floor, Beans peed on her. I took that as confirmation that she was the one he wanted and he was marking his territory. Since the kids were with me for this venture, we took a vote. It was unanimous. Everyone agreed that this little angel was coming home with us. At check out, I learned that her birthday was the same day as mine, May 29th.

Zoe was only five weeks old and weighed one pound, one ounce when we brought her home. I wasn't sure how to take care of such a young puppy, but she seemed happy eating regular dog food—that is, as long as Beans would let her.

One day, Beans walked into the kitchen and stalked up to Zoey, who was eating her meal. Beans took her little tail in his mouth and dragged her into another room. Then he literally sat on her. It was so funny that the kids and I were rolling on the floor laughing—while simultaneously trying to console little Zoey. Poor baby, it looked like we were going to have to make sure she was able to get time at the food bowl.

As it turned out, Beans did not calm down as I hoped he would after we brought Zoey home. Instead, he became aggressive, a trait I didn't want near my kids or Zoey. I had a friend, Jason England, whose mom lived on a farm with several dogs. We decided it was best to let Beans go live on the farm, where he could have the freedom to roam around the property with other dogs who shared his energy level.

When it came to naming Zoey, the choice was easy. I had always liked the name Zoey, and she was such a sweet little angel that I named her Zoey Angel. The significance of this name became evident after she passed, as I started reflecting on her life and our relationship.

When the time came for Chip to return from his military orders while we were still living in Kentucky, I was sitting on the living room floor helping the kids with a project. Little Zoey was wandering around in a small three-foot area of the floor that stretched between the desk and me. The front door was two feet directly behind me on the far right side of the room. When Chip walked through the front door, he saw a fuzzy little *Star Trek* tribble-looking fur ball. Barely avoiding stepping on her, he thought she was a toy. Poor thing, she was only half the length of his size 11 foot.

"Watch out," I shouted as I grabbed her out from under his foot. "You're about to step on her," I exclaimed as Zoey looked at me with a puzzled face. I could feel her little heart racing.

"What are you talking about? What her?" he enquired.

Then I explained that I had tried to find a friend for Beans. However, Beans did not seem to be as fond of Zoey as I had hoped. Since my 31st birthday had just passed, I told Chip that I was claiming her as a birthday gift for me. It was only a few months before I realized the significance of how special this birthday gift would be for the next twelve years and more.

During the winter of 2004, about five months after bringing Zoey home, we took that long and dreaded trip to Florida, where I received confirmation of my multiple sclerosis diagnosis. I didn't say much on the drive back to my mother-in-law's house after the appointment, but as soon as I walked through the front door, I began to sob uncontrollably. I felt as if I had just received my death sentence.

The only one I admitted into my personal space was Zoey. I didn't feel as if anyone could possibly relate to, or even comprehend, how terrified I was to face the hellacious storms I knew MS could bring. I had the sense that Zoey took my emotional breakdown as a sign that she would need to assume the caregiver role—immediately. She started licking the tears off my face. When I became so exhausted from crying that I collapsed on the floor, she crawled under my arm and lay there quietly until I picked myself up.

This little angel came to me at the start of my MS tsunami season. From the beginning, she watched as I digressed to my lowest physical, emotional, and spiritual points. Then, daily, her spirit took on so much, as she lifted me emotionally, with momentous efforts, helping me and urging me to recover from each storm this disease hurled at me.

Without words, my Zoey and I engaged in conversation all day long every day. She made me laugh with her facial and body expressions and the tilt of her head when she was pleased with something I had just said. She liked to prance up to me, jump in the air a few inches, and plop onto the ground next to me. It was as if she was sure that was her seat and she was not going to share. Although Zoey wasn't really a lap dog, she loved snuggling and she wanted to be very close. Her compromise was to tuck herself very close to my side. Sometimes it was so close that she actually managed to slide her feet under me.

"Mom.Mom.Mom.Mom.Mom!" is what I heard whenever she was excited about something I was doing for her. She let me know that I wasn't doing whatever it was fast enough. Her response was so cute that sometimes I intentionally slowed my actions, just so I could hear her say, "Mom. Mom."

While she preferred to sleep in her own bed at night, every morning she bounced onto my bed. With a swipe of her paw, she "knocked" on the "door"—my blankets. My Zoey just wanted to climb under the blankies to cuddle with her momma.

Zoey was a lover of everything I loved. For instance, when I made hot tea and had to set it down in order to walk away momentarily, I would return to find her face in my cup, gulping my tea faster than I do. I guess she wanted to make sure she had her fair share, too. Or maybe she just wanted to be like me.

She loved exploring our assortment of snack foods. When she found something wrapped in paper, she knew it had to be super-special because she recognized it as a special treat for me. She earned the nickname Purse Diver because whenever she was left alone, she would trawl around the house, looking for open purses, bags, and doors. She would hunt until she found something—anything—interesting: candy, muffins, crackers, chips, et cetera. She would highjack that tasty treat and scurry to a hiding place where she could eat it.

Once, I busted her for eating my corn muffin. When she heard me coming, she abandoned the muffin and ran to hide under a rattan side table. After I arrived in the room, I discovered her hiding place and asked her why she had put herself in jail. Then I saw a half-eaten muffin on the floor behind me and realized the answer to that question. This routine became just one of the many ways she managed to keep me laughing through the years.

When consequences of the disease consumed me and I found myself in a ball on the floor, crying my heart out, Zoey instinctively knew I needed her there beside me. She would force herself between my body and the floor just to lick the tears off my face. After I lost my sight, Zoey did not let me out of her sight except to eat and go to the bathroom. Even then, she would bring mouthfuls of food and eat next to me.

She surprised me the first day I lost my sight. Out of nowhere, she made a quiet grrrrrr sound. I was puzzled by this. Was she trying to let me know someone was coming close to me? Did she know I was blind? How did she know? I wondered.

I immediately learned that she was warning me about someone approaching. This became a pattern; during that time, she continued this response every time someone came near me. It only ended when I regained some semblance of sight.

On days when I was scheduled to have the IV steroid infusions, Zoey attempted to nurse the IV piggy back in my arm. She would lay near it and lick around it, but never on the dressing. During these days, she did not want to leave my side. She was truly one of my best caregivers through those difficult days.

As far as caregivers go, mommies are usually the best to have around. However, I'm sure you remember me sharing the story about the relationship between my mom and me. Well, my little Zoey was the polar opposite of my mother. She was my fuzzy little girl *and* my very dear mommy, who daily watched over me. I started calling her the best little momma a person could ever have.

Over the years, I've paid attention to dogs' behavioral trends. When many of them are let loose outside, they take off running, as if they are trying either to escape or go exploring. My Zoey did not do that. She always ran right back inside. On the extremely rare occasions when we accidentally shut her outdoors, she stood at the door and knocked with her little paw, letting out a series of woofs.

Zoey always let me know just how much she loved me. In fact, no one could deny our deep spiritual connection. As my physical condition continued to improve, I started watching Zoey's decline. It became my turn to repay her for the care she had so lovingly and unselfishly offered me. Several days a month, I took her to Brusters for ice cream. We also made regular visits to the beach. Those were two of her favorite activities—next to chasing squirrels.

Like her momma, Zoey loved the ocean, where she could chase birds and crabs while running out into the surf. I still remember watching the first time a crab caught the hair on Zoey's face. She swiftly shook her head to get it off. That crab went flying so high I lost sight of it! Moments later, Zoey and I both watched the crab crash on the sand about ten feet away from us. On the days Zoey actually caught a crab, she was so excited she would prance around for a minute until she saw another crab to chase. Of course, she never ate them. Hers was strictly a catch- and-release game.

I had gone for almost a year-and-a-half without needing IV steroids and medications for MS when, on Father's Day 2016, I had my first MRI in four years. While the results reflected serious prior damage, it confirmed that the disease had not progressed in the intervening years. That was something to celebrate for sure. But not for long. The following month, Zoey's health took a turn for the worse.

Our veterinarian confirmed that Zoey had heart disease and an established heart murmur. She began suffering syncope episodes that looked like she was having seizures. She uttered a loud, shrill scream every time she was about to fall over into a seizure. The scene was straight out of a horror movie, very scary. I'm sure these episodes are the things nightmares are made of. Sometimes the scream ended with the loss of her bodily functions, distressing for us all. Medication helped for about seven months, before her situation worsened.

She had to wear a heart monitor for a week. The results? When she got excited, her heartrate would drop to zero and she would fall over. Then her heartrate would jump over 200. Therefore, the vet determined that she needed a pacemaker to stabilize her heartbeats. However, she was not a good candidate for the surgery because her congestive heart failure had progressed too far. In fact, the weekend after the veterinarians removed the heart monitor, she started coughing up large amounts of clear phlegm. One Monday I contacted the vet's office with a breaking heart. We scheduled the time when Zoey would be put down. It was that Wednesday afternoon.

I opted to take her to the beach during her final days, but the scenes were very difficult for me to watch. Yet, deep down, I know that she really enjoyed that time spent with me, doing what she loved to do with the woman she loved.

As I watched the distressed look on her face, I told her that she would not have to endure the discomfort much longer. She looked at me as if she understood my words. On our last night together, my family all took her to the beach one last time. When we got home, I told her it was our last night together here. Her response? She climbed into bed with me and slept for the entire night. She did not get out of bed one time. This was not characteristic of Zoey. She had never slept in bed with us, but we knew that sometime every night she got up and trawled her food dish before scurrying to the back of the house to go to the bathroom. This pattern of activities was so regular, I could set a clock to it. However, not on our last night together.

The next morning I felt abandoned before she was even gone. My waterworks started to flow and I couldn't turn off the tears. The irony of the scene was that this time the tears Zoey licked off my face were the tears I was crying over her leaving me. I truly believe she knew that's what they were. While I hated the thought of letting her go, I knew that the decision was best for her and it was an act of love from us.

I believe if Zoey could have spoken, she would have told me, "Thank you, Momma. I hurt so badly and I'm so very tired. I really need this rest. I love you very much, and you know that I will be waiting for you at the rainbow bridge. Remember that I am always with you, Mommy."

While my heart still aches deeply as I deal with my loss, I believe from the deepest part of my spirit that Zoey took my heinous disease with her. I trust that there will be no more major progression of

241

MS in my body during my lifetime. I hope—and expect—that one day doctors will find a way to repair the damage already done. Then I will be able to live free of the effects of MS.

This was Zoey in February 2017, investigating the yellow Plumeria that I planted in her memory the day she passed. I call it my Zoey tree. Like Zoey, it will remain indoors for most of its lifetime, giving give me hope in the dark seasons of my life, just as Zoey did.

# Chapter 24
# Changing What I Could.

Throughout this book, you have heard me reflect on multiple situations that I had no control over. When we are faced with situations that we cannot control, it can leave us feeling hopeless and defeated. I'm sure you picked up on the moments where I shared these feelings in my storms. Most recently was saying goodbye to my dear companion, Zoey.

The truth is that no matter what situation we find ourselves, we do have the power to make positive changes to our circumstances. In order to accomplish this, we much start with a desire to change our current situations and followup with commitment to that change.

To change circumstances within each of my storms, I address three main a facets. The first were physical requirements for life which include physical and safety needs. Second was social influences, self-actualization, and mindset to always stay positive. Lastly, I identified my desire for change, then I changed the things I could.

I was continually on a search for the best and safest place to live. As you saw, I went as far as changing houses and states. This was followed by researching and discussing with physicians the best food choices that would help strengthen my body and aid it in fighting for itself.

In the process of adding the right foods, I removed foods and activies that were not healthy, like sodas, deep fried foods, and smoking. Once I gave my body the proper energy through food and removed unwanted chemical consumption, I added the element of exercise. These activities collectively helped me to gain better sleep.

Once I reached my basic needs I focused on self esteme and relationships. Sometimes my storms were so difficult that I had to revert back to self-esteme issues before I could establish my basic needs. Earlier in the book, you saw that my nuclear family has been broken since almost since the beginning. In my desire and need to have family, I reached out to friends and eventually learned that sometimes, our family does not share the same blood line. At the end of the day, blood lines do not matter.

I'm sure you may be asking why we did not have family involved during my many crises. The answer is, we did. The only member of my family involved was my dad, after he finally called me and learned of the situation. Chip must have been too deep in crisis mode that he never called him. All of my family lives out of state in the north.

As for local family, that is Chip's family. They were here and did know about my circumstances but not immediately because Chip's main focus was getting me medical attention. I do not really have words to describe his family. But I can say, for those who were in proximity, they helped as best they could which explains why I felt so isolated.

One of my major lifesavors was mindset. I did not have to rely on external sources to harness this inner strength. While my immediate response seems to be sheer panic and doubt, after mauling over details I can quickly reset to optimism. Mindset for me is the charge I use to make changes to the things I can. While there are many, let me offer a couple significant examples.

The first was in my youth. This was a time when I felt no personal value and reflected that in the worst self talk imaginable. I had to identify with the lost little, no named, girl deep within who was screaming for help. She had value that was priceless and worth fighting for. At the risk of sounding like I had a dual personality, I will confess that it was the lost little girl, not me that I was fighting for. It was her value I was fighting for, not mine. Maybe some day I will resolve my past by realizing she was me and I did have value in my youth.

With my mental energy, I saw the right moment and harnessed every thread of my person to blindly jump off the ship into the deep end of the water and wade to safety at my dad's house. This would not have been possible if I was weak in mind for that weakness it what kept me there so many years.

The second involves my name. On the cover of this book you see the name Phoebe and in the text of the book you see Gretchen. As far back as I can remember I have not liked my name. Often times, especially in the storms, I found comfort in giving myself a new name.

As a small child, I remember laying with my grandmother on her couch watching beauty pageants. As she combed her fingers through my hair I would talk of how much I did not like my name. She reminded me how she tried to stop my mother from giving me that name because it sounded too scratchy for a beautiful young girl to have. Then we would watch the pretty ladies walk across the stage.

As we identified one with a really pretty name, she proclaimed, "One day that will be you." I knew back then, even before my major trials, that one day I would actually change my name. For years, I've allowed myself to secretly try on new names while I waited for the right time to present itself.

Through my many storms, I learned that sometimes we become empowered when we make changes to significant parts of ourselves. One of these was my decision to have the prophylactic mastectomy and hysterectomy. Then as I wrote my book and reflected on the vast number of trials I have survived, I felt like the time to make the change was approaching.

The name, Phoebe, was not easy to find and did not come overnight. It was a process that took years. Once I determined the name and the right time to make the shift, I needed to test the waters with the new name before making it official. While it is not official yet, Phoebe is the name you see on the cover of my books and it is associated with all details regarding my business, Silverliningsfyi, LLC. It is my prefered name and the official change is coming soon.

Of the changes I've elected for myself, my name change has brought the most healing to my soul. I am now 44-years-old. You've seen in this book where the majority of my life has been in crisis mode. I believe it was a time to shut the door on the patterns of the past and break open the seal to a new path for my future. I feel like I am giving myself permission, not to forget about my past, where I came from, and who I am, but to shut the door to ever letting the past resurface in the future. It has no place or control here. The control is mine and I feel stronger by being able to make such a tremendous legal decision for myself. I feel more confident and empowered to make many more positive changes for myself in the future, where ever it takes me.

Phoebe Walker

# Chapter 25
# Where to From Here?

Clearly, my life path has taken me through many tremendous highs and lows. How can I top them? Do I attempt to?

No.

I believe the highs and lows are the steppingstones that led to the creation of the person I am today. While I have had horrific trials, as difficult as they were and as strange as it is to say, I would not deny any of them. It seems that the greater the trial I walked through, the greater the fulfillment and reward on the other side. Additionally, the various walks I have taken have opened opportunities for me to offer hope and inspiration to others going through similar—or equally difficult—situations.

I find that some of my greatest satisfaction in life comes from walking with friends, acquaintances, and even strangers going through similar hardships. I found it much easier to walk through a trial with someone who understood pain, suffering, and loss, because they knew the right things to say and do. Walking alongside someone who had survived great trials offered me guidance and hope. I aim to offer the same gifts to others.

Earlier in the book, I talked about my desires to study biology and also attend seminary. However, my medical challenges and achievements do not totally define the woman I am today. Nor do they offer a precise direction for my future. In fact, I do not believe I can determine my future without considering all the factors that define me.

I am a mother with no more chick-lings in the roost to raise. I feel complete when I am able to do many things at once: utilize my creative side, draw on my intellectual side, and serve as an inspiration to others, especially my husband and kids. Maybe this multi-faceted persona *IS* an indicator of my purpose and direction.

Separate from what I do in life is who I am in this world. My deepest desire is to maintain peace and joy here on earth. In my definition, that means a place where people do not oppose each other. Rather, they join in a mutual cause: to live the best life physically, spiritually, and emotionally, that they can achieve. I believe we accomplish this by treating all humanity as equals.

I imagine that my love for people is the reason I enjoy cruises so much. The people who work onboard a ship do so side-by-side with people they might not otherwise associate with because of their countries' laws. Those are human-created boundaries. The people who cruise have the opportunity to leave the stresses of life at home and allow themselves downtime to relax. This opportunity for relaxation encourages us all to treat ourselves to a much-deserved rest, to be good to ourselves for a change, and even to share familial love with complete strangers. I believe this exudes the perfect picture of our spiritual design and purpose on earth.

My trials were both massive and difficult. But as I walked, stumbled, collapsed, and rose from them, I knew in my heart that hard times come to us all as we progress through life. None of us is exempt, and we should not want to be. By design, trials make us stronger, wiser, and more empathetic to others—if we let them. Trials also make our personal stories full and complete. Maybe my greatest challenge should not be merely surviving these times, but focusing on how I will celebrate each of the trials as I overcome them.

As for direction, I do not need to know a physical destination. We should not attempt to see farther than what the present light illuminates. Seeing the entire picture would be entirely too overwhelming.

I have MS, but it does not define who I am and what I can or cannot do. I am still functional, though at times I need to lean on other people or devices to maintain that ability. As long as I remember to be honest about my current condition, the necessary crutches will find their way to me as they are needed – my silver linings.

I believe sharing my story is the best place to start. As for the specific decisions about how my career will take shape in the future, I will just go where the spirit leads me. If it is a position in the field of biology, I will take it. Likewise, if it is a spiritual/theological position, I will take that.

I imagine there will be seasons for both.

Now that I have shared where I have been, who I am, and who I aim to become, I want to conclude with this final thought on my life's calling.

It is highly probable, thanks to the number and magnitude of trials I have walked through, that my call is to share my plethora of stories through motivational speaking. I believe it may help people find hope after hearing about how one person survived—and flourished— through difficult times. My stories stress that I could not and did not find success on my own. I was never alone. I always had loving family members, helpful strangers, and great friends along the way—and they have been my silver linings.

In fact, as I reflect on what I have written, I realize another common thread originated when I began suffering from severe mental, emotional, and physical abuse, as well as their consequences. The abuse started in my early years, when I was exposed to things a girl my age—or any age—should ever experience. The abuse led to irrational thinking, which manifested itself in bad behavioral choices. My season of promiscuity led to pregnancies at a young age. Motherhood caused me to mature more quickly into an adult without fully progressing through my juvenile stages—and that left me undeveloped, or underdeveloped, in many ways. I had some major catching-up to do.

Once I started having children, my heart's desire was to have several girls. Perhaps that was because I wanted to re-do my youth by living vicariously through daughters. I could give them everything I lacked, while protecting them from harm. Or so I thought. When Chip and I went to adopt, we requested a girl between the ages of seven and fifteen. Many years later, an epiphany came to me while I was writing this section. I was seven years old when my parents divorced, and I was fifteen when I moved in with my dad. I don't believe our choice of that age range was a coincidence.

I strongly believe my future is, in some form, going to consist of walking with women victims of abuse—women of all ages. I am ready for that challenge, and I look forward to it. I hope I can help liberate these women and encourage them to live joyful, fulfilling lives. Just as I have.

Phoebe Walker

# Epilogue

I am starting to forget the precise feeling I had the very moment when I first felt the angel sitting next to me in my living room during some of my darkest days. I continue to feel humbled by the deep conviction that I sat in the presence of a divine spirit that day in 2006. Please don't misunderstand. I do not want to return to that place again in order to refresh that memory. However, once you experience something so intensely spiritual, nothing else on this earth can match its majesty, beauty, and power. NOTHING!

While reading this book, I am sure you noticed a common process I went through repeatedly:

* Tragedy happened.
* I wondered what caused it.
* I feared I would never get better.
* I asked what my next step should be, and where help would come from.
* Then I gained a forward momentum.
* Perseverance—as well as my silver linings—guided me through the process.

* I survived each storm, feeling stronger and wiser and more appreciative at the end.

Now that I know where to look for my silver linings, I do not have an excuse to stay down when things get difficult—and getting up is the key to survival!

Humanity is plagued by trials and hardships. Some will be our personal trials; others will be trials where we watch helplessly as those we love struggle mightily. In these times, we can expect to be crushed and broken.

While writing my first book, I talked to my daughter about how badly it felt to be broken and crushed. I heard her say, "Mom, think about how the most intense pressure creates a diamond. Once the diamond is created, it is very solid and virtually impossible to crush. Maybe if we think of our trials as a means to create diamonds in our lives, we can hold out through that refiner's fire long enough to become that beautiful diamond. Diamonds sparkle in the light. They're beautiful to look at and bright enough to illuminate hidden facets of our lives."

After writing this in my first book, my daughter approached me to say that was not what she actually she said, but she felt my interpretation was really neat. I love how sometimes we may not hear things correctly, but we hear what we need to.

Regardless of my emotional rollercoaster ride, my life walk has transformed me from a victim to a victor. I am a survivor who thrives through perseverance. Sometimes things just happen. That's life. No matter whether we find ourselves in a tough life walk or under attack—physical or perceived, we must trust that no matter how bleak or desperate our situation appears to be, we can always rely on our faith for respite and resolve.

Our attitudes and responses to our current life situations play a tremendous role in determining whether we will ultimately find success or failure at the end of the story. For instance, in the moments when I felt like a victim, I displayed some hefty emotional diarrhea. The moment I relied upon my faith, I gained a strength that could take down mighty creatures—and problems. As long as I get up as many times as I get knocked down, then I become victorious. I will continue to persevere in life. No matter what seemingly uncontrollable obstacles or challenges we face, *we* control our responses and our attitudes. If they're positive, the outcome will be positive.

I choose life—it's worth fighting for!

# Appendix A

## My Webpage and blog for this book:

## www.silverliningsfyi.com

---

## My Research Site:

## www.seafwa.org

Search proceedings under publications

For – Gretchen E. Walker **(case sensitive)**

---

## My Surfboard location:

Madd Jacks Grillin Shack

Cocoa Beach, FL

www.maddjacksgrillinshack.com

# APPENDIX B

## Breast Cancer Links I used:

1. National Breast Cancer Foundation, Inc. - http://www.nationalbreastcancer.org/

2. National Breast Cancer Foundation, Inc. Donations - https://www.nationalbreastcancer.org/breast-cancer-donations

3. Susan G. Komen Breast Cancer Foundation - http://ww5.komen.org/

4. The Center for Restorative Breast Surgery (Where surgeons performed my double mastectomy and reconstruction)- http://www.breastcenter.com/

5. 1717 St. Charles Avenue New Orleans, LA 70130 | Tel: 504.899.2800 | Fax: 504.899.2700 | Toll Free: 888.899.2288| info@breastcenter.com

## Multiple Sclerosis:

1. National Multiple Sclerosis Society - http://www.nationalmssociety.org/

2. For donations to the Multiple Sclerosis society - http://www.nationalmssociety.org/Donate

3. Dr. Scott Gold (My neurologist) - http://scottlgold.md.com/
   321-725-4500

   1223 Gateway Drive Suite 2G, Melbourne, FL 32901
   and
   7125 Murrell Road Suite F, Melbourne, FL 32940

## Lou Gehrig's Disease:

Lou Gehrig's ALS Association – http://www.alsa.org/about-als/what-is-als.html

# Churches:

1.  Indian River City United Methodist Church (IRC)

    www.ircumc.com

    1355 Cheney Hwy, Titusville, FL 32780 – Phone: (321) 267-7922

2.  St. Gabriel's Episcopal Church

    www.stgabriels.church

    414 Pine St, Titusville, FL 32796 –Phone: (321) 267-2545

# Chiropractor/Acupuncturist:

Daly Chiropractic and Wellness Center

http://dalywellnesscenter.com/

2708 Garden St, Titusville, FL 32796 · (321) 267-4324

# Appendix C

---

## Two of Robin's Poetry Pieces

### BRANCHES OF GOD'S TREE
We are branches of a large unimaginable tree
We bear fruit in many colors for all to see.

Our roots grow strong where they belong,
Beneath that heavenly trunk.
We delight in nourishing others
With all the nectar they have drunk.

We are branches of a large unimaginable tree.
We bear fruit in many colors for all to see.

It is so sad when a branch is bad.
It withers and rots on the ground.
We shake our leaves and pray for them,
But they are lost, never to be found.

We are branches of a large unimaginable tree.
We bear fruit in many colors for all to see.

It's a sign to us to see other leaves rust
As they bear fruit no more.

But we check our roots in God's pursuits,
And make sure they remain secure.

We are all branches of a large unimaginable tree.
We bear fruit in many colors for all to see.

We all have the chance when we see a glance
From a lost and needy soul
To fill their cups with love and trust,
For that is our eternal goal.

We are all branches of a large unimaginable tree.
We bear fruit in many colors for all to see.

## ARMS OPEN WIDE
I'm standing here, arms open wide,
Letting Jesus deep inside.
We will both walk side by side,
Enjoying life's roller coaster ride.
Up and down,
Round and round.

No matter how far we go,
I am safe because I know,
High and low,
Fast and slow,
I'm facing life full speed ahead.

263

There is nothing that I dread,
Quiet and loud,
Humble not proud.
I'm facing life full circle now.

Thanks to God who taught me how
To stand here, arms open wide,
And let Jesus deep inside.
We will both walk side by side.
Now life's a smooth roller coaster ride.

# Appendix D

# Vow renewal

## WEDDING PROGRAM
### March 24th, 2007

**1. Three sounds from the conch shell:**
This marks the beginning of the ceremony and signifies the presence of the holy trinity.

**2. Lei exchange:**
A Hawaiian wedding often begins with the lei exchange for several different reasons.
One is that the Lei is a circle, like the rings that are worn representing the eternal commitment and unbroken devotion of your hearts to each other.
Another is that each individual flower that is woven into the Lei loses none of its individual beauty when it forms the circle. Its beauty is enhanced. Likewise, in your marriage you do not compromise or lose your individual identity and unique beauty.

**3. Opening**

**4. Vows**

**5. Exchange of rings**

- Wait, we've already done that, so we are going to do two other ceremonies instead.

First will be a blessing of our hands, followed by a lasso ceremony. The lasso is draped in a figure 8 around our wrists by the pastor signifying eternity of our love and marriage. This ceremony will conclude with a recommitment to our marriage.

### 6. Unity candle time

Ok, so we can't light candles on a windy beach. In its place, we chose to do a sand ceremony. From this day forward, we will have this beautiful sand jar to remind us about how beautifully we blend.

### 7. Conclusion including wreath ceremony...

We will remove the leis that we have been wearing and carry them to the ocean. Tradition says that if we take them to the ocean and offer them out to our deceased relatives/friends, when they come back, we, as the happy couple, will have received the blessing of those deceased relatives/friends. We will also perform a wreath ceremony at this time. We take a wreath, which represents trials, hurts, failures, etc. of our time together and offer them up to God by sending the wreath out to sea. Tradition says that when the wreath comes back, we've been cleansed of all those hard times/trails, hurts, failures, etc.

Then we get to kiss again... YAY! Then you all, our guests, may go upstairs to the reception room while we clean up the beach and take photos.

**Mahalo nui loa na ho'olaule'a me la kaua. Ua ola loko I ke aloha.
(Thank you for celebrating with us. Love gives life within.)**

# The Service:

Blow in the conch shell three times (signifying the presence of the holy trinity) then the pastor will say a prayer.

Pastor hand Chip a lei to place on Gretchen with a kiss and hand Gretchen a lei to place on Chip with a kiss.

## OPENING:

**(Brenda)** Good relationships never stop growing. Like fine wine, they get better with age. Chip and Gretchen, you have now been married for ten years, and through all of the years of your journey together, you have now come to this beautiful setting, so that you can renew your vow and commitment of love for each other.

No marriage is perfect. As you continue in this union, you already know that it will continue to take a lot of love and work to keep your relationship an ongoing success. Many couples tend to think of marriage as a 50/50 proposition. Actually, the best relationships are 90/10. If you both will give 90% and take only 10%, you will have a formula likely to continue to bring both of you happiness for a lifetime.

As you continue on your journey together, I ask you to remember this advice:

- Let your love be stronger than your anger.
- Learn the wisdom of compromise, for it is better to bend than to break.
- Believe the best of your beloved rather than the worst.
- Confide in your partner and ask for help when you need it.
- Remember that true friendship is the basis for any lasting relationship. Give your spouse the same courtesies and kindnesses you bestow on your friends. Say, "I love you" every day.

Chip and Gretchen, I remind you that marriage is a precious gift, a lifelong dedication to love and a daily challenge to love one another more fully and more freely.

With this understanding, do you Chip, continue to take Gretchen as your beloved wife? Will you continue to be a tender faithful husband, continue to love and cherish her, in sickness and health, for richer, for poorer, for better, for worse, and keep yourself only unto her?

With this understanding, do you Gretchen, continue to take Chip as your beloved husband, continue to love and cherish him, in sickness and health, for richer, for poorer, for better, for worse, and keep yourself only unto him?

# VOWS:

**(Pastor)** say a prayer.

Eternal God, creator and preserver of all life, author of salvation, giver of all grace, bless Chip and Gretchen, who come now to recommit themselves in holy marriage. Grant that they may give their vows to each other in the strength of your steadfast love. Enable them to continue growing in love and peace with you and with one another all the days of their lives. Amen.

**(Chip to Gretchen)**

You glow with an inner and outer beauty. Your smile melts the toughest situation, and your embrace warms me up on the coldest night. When I look at you, I see a person confident in herself, who glows in any circumstance, whose fortitude and strength allows you to remain grounded in God when the storms come. I see a heart aching to help others, a heart that is able to conquer a situation that most would have withdrawn from. You overextend yourself due to kindness, and rely on God and me to carry you through. Your faith is childlike in belief and growing with hunger through each experience and day. You clearly have a light lit by the Lord. You live to have joy in each day. You challenge me to be a better husband, father, and man. You have touched the inner parts of my heart and soul that only God has been able to reach and dwell. This has caused me to be the man who stands before you, and I am very happy with whom I have become. You are my biggest supporter, and I confide all things in you. You are the other half of my heart, and complete me in every way. Being connected with you so deeply and emotionally ensures that you can both give me my greatest feelings of joy and deepest hurt. You make my heart skip a beat every time I come home and see you smile when you see me, even ten years later. You cause my heart to ache when I see you in pain and anguish. I want to hold you, fix it all, wrap my arms around you, and prevent anything and everyone from hurting you. All of these God-Blessed traits make me feel undeserving of you. I am blessed that God has allowed us to share our lives together.

**(Gretchen to Chip)**

You are my best friend, with whom I share my dreams, playtime, and prayer time. I share my everything with you. In you, I can see a breath-taking image of God's love for me. He was incredible in how he created only you for me, how you loved me endlessly when I could not even find myself. You tried to put my pieces back together to make me whole again. You've held my hand in the darkness and numbness to pull me back into the light of Christ. We have endured excessive trials together with great strength and victory – as God has intended. I love you with my entire soul and spirit, a place that only you and God may reside! Thank you for marrying me again. My vow to you is that I can give back to you all that you are and all that you have given me—and much, more, with the help of God. I love you.

**(Brenda)** Chip and Gretchen have rings as the outward symbols of their ongoing commitment to each other. From earliest times, the ring has been a symbol of wedded love. An unbroken and never-ending circle symbolizes a commitment to love that is also never ending. Chip and Gretchen have decided to do hand blessing and lasso ceremonies in place of the ring exchange, because they already exchanged rings ten years ago.

## HAND BLESSING CEREMONY:

(Pastor) Gretchen, please hold Chip's hands palms up, so you may see the gift that they have been and are to you.

These are the hands of your best friend, young and strong and vibrant with love, that is holding yours on this day, as he promises to continue passionately loving and cherishing you through the years, for a lifetime of happiness.

These are the hands that have and will continue to work alongside yours, as together you continue to build your future, as you laugh and cry as you share your innermost secrets and dreams.

These are the hands that have, and will continue to, countless times wipe the tears from your eyes: tears of sorrow and tears of joy.

These are the hands that have and will continue to comfort you in illness, and hold you when fear or grief engulfs your heart.

These are the hands that when wrinkled and aged will still be reaching for yours, still giving you the same unspoken tenderness with just a touch..

These are the hands that will tenderly lift your chin and brush your cheek as they raise your face to look into his eyes: eyes that are filled completely with his overwhelming love and desire for you.

Chip, please hold Gretchen's hands palms up, so you may see the gift that they are to you.

These are the hands of your best friend, smooth, young and carefree, that are holding yours on this day, as she promises to continue passionately loving and cherishing you through the years, for a lifetime of happiness.

These are the hands that have and will continue to massage tension from you neck and back in the evenings after you've both had a long hard day.

These are the hands that have and will continue to hold you tight as you struggle through difficult times.

These are the hands that have and will continue to comfort you when you are sick, or console you when you are grieving.

These are the hands that when wrinkled and aged will still be reaching for yours, still giving you the same unspoken tenderness with just a touch.

These are the hands that will give you support as she encourages you to chase down your dreams.

Together as a team, everything you wish for can be realized and attained with the help of God.

## LASSO CEREMONY:

(**Pastor**, place the lasso around Chip and Gretchen's wrists in a figure eight while explaining the following)

The lasso, placed around the wrists of Chip and Gretchen, and shaped in an infinity symbol, symbolizes their love and eternity of marriage. Both Chip and Gretchen must equally shoulder the responsibilities that a marriage brings. They pledge to support each other in love, joy and sorrow.

Chip repeat after me – From this day on, I recommit myself to you, your ring and this lasso are symbols of my pledge.

Gretchen repeat after me - From this day on, I recommit myself to you, your ring and this lasso are symbols of my pledge.

God, bless these hands that you see before you this day. May they always be held by one another. Give them the strength to hold on during the storms of stress and the dark of disillusionment. Keep them tender and gentle as they nurture each other in their wondrous love. Help these hands to continue building a relationship founded in your grace, rich in caring, and devoted in reaching for your perfection. May Chip and Gretchen see their four hands as healer, protector, shelter and guide. We ask this in Jesus name, Amen.

## SAND BLENDING CEREMONEY:

**(Brenda)**

Chip and Gretchen, may your love always be as constant as the never-ending waves, flowing endlessly from the depths of the sea. Just as the waters touch and nourish the many shores of the earth, may your love be a moving sea between the shores of your souls. Just as there will never be a morning without the ocean's flow, there will never be a day without your love for each other.

The first shell represents you Chip, in all that you were, all that you are as part of a couple, and all that you will ever be, and the other shell represents you Gretchen, in all that you were, all that you are as part of a couple and all that you will ever be. The brown sand in the bottom of the bottle represents Christ, who is your life's foundation. Each one holds its own unique beauty, strength, and character. They can stand on their own with Christ and be whole, without need of anything else. However, after these three are blended together they will create an entirely new and extraordinarily more intricate entity. Each grain of sand brings to the mixture a lasting beauty that forever enriches the combination.

Please pour the sand into this common container to symbolize your oneness.

This container of sand represents the last ten years and your future lives together. Just as these grains of sand can never be separated and poured again into the individual containers, so is your marriage a molding of two individual personalities, bonded together forming one heart and one love in Christ.

Walk the leis to the ocean and toss them out to share this day with your deceased relatives and friends. Place the wreath in the ocean with all of your combined past trials, hardships, pain, and disappointments of the past. Allow Christ to take them, freeing yourselves, from this day forward, of old baggage. Out with the old. In with the new.

May the sun bring you new energy by day. May the moon softly restore you by night. May the rain wash away your worries. And may you live the days of your lives in peace, love, and happiness.

(Pastor) you may choose to add a prayer here if you'd like... your choice
Chip and Gretchen, having witnessed your vows of affirmation with God, all who are assembled here, and by the authority of love itself, I do affirm that you have expressed your desire to continue as husband and wife.

You may now kiss your bride.

Ladies and Gentleman, it is my honor to present to you, once again as husband and wife: Lieutenant Commander and Mrs. Chip Walker

Thank you for reading. I hope you enjoyed my story and found hope from what you've read.

If you want to contact me, go to:

www.silverliningsfyi.com

or e-mail me at

phoebe.walker@silverliningsfyi.com

My friend Wanda took family photos for us December 2014. My family from left to right, Ryan, Phoebe, Ashley, TJ, Chip